New Light on the Difficult Words of Jesus
Insights from His Jewish Context

David Bivin

Edited by Lois Tverberg & Bruce Okkema

Foreword by Dwight A. Pryor

En-Gedi Resource Center
EnGediResourceCenter.com

Printed in the United States of America

Design by Bruce Okkema

Library of Congress Cataloging-in-Publication Data:
Library of Congress Control Number: 2005929588

ISBN 978-0-9749482-2-5

Printed in the United States of America

To
Dolly MacDonald,

whose devotion to the quest for a more accurate
understanding of Jesus' words made the research
for this book possible.

Contents

II. Jesus' First-Century Jewish Context

III. New Light on Jesus' Teachings

IV. The Kingdom Is Here

List of Illustrations

Foreword
Dwight A. Pryor

Every year countless Christians journey up to Jerusalem from the nations to see where their Lord lived and died. With the assistance of Israel's outstanding guides, these excited pilgrims eagerly explore the land and the places where Jesus walked; they peer out their bus windows into his Jewish world, and they meet his brethren after the flesh, the Jewish people.

Invariably these faithful followers of Christ the Lord find their faith deepened by the experience of Israel — its Land, its People, and its Scriptures.

I know. More than twenty years ago, a journey up to Jerusalem forever changed my life. I came on an extended study tour of Israel that introduced me to a remarkable team of scholars living in the Land.

These men and women — both Christians and Jews — together were excavating as it were the words of Jesus preserved so beautifully for us in the Synoptic (parallel) Gospels of Matthew, Mark and Luke. Their collective insights opened a portal into the first-century Jewish world of Jesus that enabled me to see the Master in a brilliant new light. Not only was he the risen Messiah and Savior — known to me already in a transforming personal way — but he also was a Jewish rabbi or sage. Here in Israel I met the man, the historical Jesus of Nazareth. I encountered *Rav Yeshua* (the Rabbi Jesus).

The first Jerusalem scholar that I met on that fateful excursion into Jesus' Jewish world was David Bivin. He became a dear friend, a mentor and colleague in the continuing quest for new insights into the words, the wisdom and the world of the One we call Lord. Two decades later I continue to learn from David's perceptive research, and count it a privilege to sit at table with him, discussing the Scriptures and the Sage who taught them authoritatively and embodied them incarnationally.

In this stimulating collection of writings, *New Light on the Difficult Words of Jesus*, David Bivin offers you an opportunity that few have enjoyed: He will be your personal tour guide through the multi-hued Jewish landscape that frames the words of our Lord!

On this tour you will glimpse the world of the sages of Israel, the great teachers of the Torah (Law), and the subtle and sophisticated teaching methods they use to explicate the Word of God. You will hear Jesus speak in his native tongue of Hebrew, and feel what it was like to be "covered in the dust" of this gifted first-century rabbi. You will explore the culture and better understand the context of Jesus' life and ministry as a man, and gain precious insights into his pre-eminent and pervasive teaching: the Kingdom of Heaven (God).

Few guides are better equipped to show you these exciting vistas. Bivin's insights into the life and times of Messiah are nuggets mined from a lifetime of labor, with scholarly skill and faithful determination.

As the Son of Man, Jesus was destined to go up to Jerusalem and be handed over to a Roman cross. But as a man, his mission from God was to raise up many disciples, teaching them the ways of the God of Israel and His in-breaking redemptive reign in the person and work of *Yeshua MiNatzeret* (Jesus of Nazareth).

This is the Jesus you will encounter on this study tour with David Bivin. It may change your life. It did mine. I came to Jerusalem as a believer in Jesus. I left determined to become a disciple of *Rav Yeshua*.

Reading *New Light on the Difficult Words of Jesus* will increase your love and respect for the man, Jesus, and summon your heart to walk after him in paths of discipleship. And that will be to the praise of his Father's glory.

Dwight A. Pryor is Founder and President of the Center for Judaic-Christian Studies in Dayton, Ohio and Jerusalem, Israel, and a founding member of the Jerusalem School of Synoptic Research.

Editors' Preface

Two thousand years after they were first spoken, in a language twice removed from our own, Jesus' words are often difficult. They come out of a foreign culture, they go against the grain of our instincts, and they challenge us to do very difficult things – to love the unlovable and care for our enemies.

We have tended to read the teachings of Jesus as if they can be removed from any context, making them timeless and universal. Because of Jesus' divinity, we tend to forget that these words were spoken by a man who lived in a particular place and time. But we find that devoid of context, his words can sometimes be cryptic and strange. Or, we might think we understand clearly, but a deeper message escapes us because we don't see how Jesus was brilliantly commenting on ideas from his time.

What if we were to read his words in light of the Jewish literature of his period, considering that he was part of a larger discussion going on around him? Even though his sayings will make more sense, it may bother us that some aspects of Jesus' life were not so unusual in his time. Others wandered the land preaching, telling parables, and training disciples, sometimes even giving messages similar to his. It takes faith to keep studying in this manner, not knowing if our convictions about his uniqueness will be affirmed.

About ten years ago, we started this journey of learning more about Jesus in his Jewish context for ourselves. Initially we were skeptical of whether any good could come out of such a study that might threaten our long-held understanding of Jesus. But what we found was just the opposite – when we heard his teachings in the context of his world, many "ah-hah's!" and satisfying answers emerged for questions that we had been almost afraid to ask, and his powerful words became much more applicable to our lives. Hearing Jesus' message with new clarity confirmed our belief in him as our Messiah and Lord, and so enriched our faith that it compelled us to begin the ministry of the En-Gedi Resource Center.

In the middle of this discovery process we met David Bivin, a scholar who was publishing a wonderful magazine called *Jerusalem Perspective*, full of rich nuggets of insight that he and others had unearthed about the Gospels in their first-century Jewish context. We studied with David during many seminars that challenged us to listen to Jesus through Jewish ears, and along the way we became close friends. In that time, we have seen this Jesus reflected in his own life.

David's lifetime of research with noted scholars of rabbinic literature, Semitic languages, ancient texts, and archaeology has yielded innumerable insights that he has shared through *Jerusalem Perspective*. Many of the articles in *JP* have been foundational in our understanding of Jesus but have never been published in book form. For years we have wished that this information could be more widely available, and now our ministry feels privileged to share with you the Jesus that David has shared with us.

The intention of this book is to give people *knowledge* of Jesus, in the Hebraic sense of the word. Rather than being purely factual and academic, we desire to let people know him relationally and experientially, as a disciple would, after walking in his footsteps for many years. In the first section we introduce the reality of Jesus as a Jewish rabbi, showing his heart for teaching and his high expectations of his disciples, and therefore us. Next we look at how Jewish he was, utterly a part of his first-century world, rather than being opposed to it, as many have believed. And then we look at the Jewishness of his teaching — how he used rabbinic terms and logic, and how his words are greatly clarified by hearing them in the context of other rabbinic sayings of his time. Finally, we share some ideas on life in his Kingdom — living out our calling as engrafted members of the Olive Tree of Israel, of which he is the "Righteous Branch"!

The Editors

Preface

David Bivin

Much of what I share in this book is not new. It was known already in the nineteenth and early twentieth centuries by scholars such as Edwin A. Abbott, Israel Abrahams, C. F. Burney, Gustaf Dalman, C. G. Montefiore, Charles C. Torrey, and even earlier by the pioneering giants, John Gill and John Lightfoot.

Biblical scholars such as these had a thorough knowledge of all the biblical languages: Hebrew, Aramaic and Greek. Their penetrating comments on the inspired text flowed from intimate familiarity with the wellsprings of rabbinic literature, as well as other first-century Jewish sources, particularly the Apocrypha and Pseudepigrapha. Indeed, their knowledge of original languages and Second Temple-period Jewish literature equipped them to make groundbreaking discoveries and draw important conclusions, now confirmed by the exciting discovery of the Dead Sea Scrolls.

My research into the life and language of our Lord is the fruit of sitting at the feet of similarly brilliant Christian and Jewish scholars in Jerusalem for more than forty years. These include distinguished and knowledgeable professors at the Hebrew University, such as David Flusser and Samuel Safrai (both of blessed memory) and the zestful and creative Dr. Robert Lindsey, my pastor for three decades (also of blessed memory). I have gleaned a great deal from shared investigations with learned fellow members of the Jerusalem School of Synoptic Research, and even more, in some ways, from the wisdom of students that I have been privileged to teach. As Rabbi Hanina said, "I have learned a lot from my teachers; from my colleagues, more than from my teachers; but, from my students, more than from all of them" (b. Ta'anit 7a). To them all I am indebted, and to them all I am deeply grateful.

There are many others to whom I owe a debt of thanks for making this book possible, firstly, to my wife Josa — for her endless patience, love and faithfulness. Other family members and friends, too numerous to mention, have donated sacrificially over the years to keep my research and writing alive. May their reward be in Heaven! Jeffrey Magnuson, the talented first editor of *Jerusalem Perspective* magazine, and Joseph Frankovic, his skilled successor, as well as many members of our local community who volunteered endless hours assembling and mailing out issues of *"JP"* – without them surely we would not have reached this point.

Finally, a double portion of thanks go to Bruce Okkema and Lois Tverberg of the En-Gedi Resource Center for creatively initiating, compiling, editing and publishing *New Light on the Difficult Words of Jesus*.

ברוך שהחיינו וקימנו והגיענו לזמן הזה!

(Blessed is He who has kept us alive, preserved us,
and brought us to this time!)

Abbreviations

Many of the abbreviations used in this book should be familiar to the general reader. Below is a partial list of abbreviations to serve as a convenient reference.

1QS	*Manual of Discipline*, a text of the Essene sect found in the Dead Sea Scrolls*
Antiq.	*Jewish Antiquities* (a work of Josephus)
b.	Babylonian, as in Babylonian Talmud*
c.	*circa*, (Latin) "about," referring to an approximate date
cf.	*confer* (Latin), meaning "compare"
e.g.	*exempli gratia* (Latin), meaning "for example"
i.e.	*id est* (Latin), "that is," meaning that an explanation follows
ibid.	*ibidem* (Latin), "the same," meaning the same work as just cited
j.	Jerusalem, as in Jerusalem Talmud*
JPS	The English translation of the Hebrew Scriptures by the Jewish Publication Society
KJV	King James Version
LXX	Septuagint*
m.	Mishnah*
NASB	New American Standard Bible
NIV	New International Version
NT	New Testament
OT	Old Testament
RSV	Revised Standard Version

Sir   Sirach, a book of the Apocrypha*
t.   Tosephta*
TDNT   Theological Dictionary of the New Testament
War   *The Jewish War*, (a work of Josephus)

Note: Unless otherwise indicated, quotations from Scripture, rabbinic literature and other Second Temple-period sources are the author's own translations.

* See the Glossary for further explanation of this term.

Introduction: A New Approach to Understanding Jesus

The Editors

Even though Christians have historically sought to define themselves apart from their Jewish background and have emphasized their differences with that faith, interest in the Jewish context of the Bible is hardly new. Theologians from Thomas Aquinas to the early American church fathers have consulted rabbinic commentaries to understand the Hebrew Scriptures.[1] Nevertheless, the traditional Christian understanding of Jesus has been that he broke away from Jewish religious traditions to teach something entirely new, and that therefore, Jewish sources are not useful for understanding his words.

In the past half century, however, there has been a new interest among Christians in studying Jesus' world of first-century Judaism, a period critical to the history of both Christians and Jews. Scholars who have compared Jesus' teachings to his contemporaries are seeing that rather than being entirely antagonistic to their ideology, Jesus' teaching brilliantly built upon the thinking of his time and brought it to a new level. A realization is now taking place among Christians that when we listen to his teachings within their Jewish context, we gain a fuller, deeper understanding of his message. This new interest is strongly linked to recent archaeological finds and the discovery of ancient texts in the past century, especially the Dead Sea Scrolls. These new sources of data have vastly increased scholars' ability to reconstruct Jesus' Second Temple Jewish context, and hold great potential for shedding light on the setting of his ministry.

This book, *New Light on the Difficult Words of Jesus*, is the fruit of one scholar's effort to re-situate Jesus in his Jewish world, and then to reexamine his teachings in light of that context. Most chapters are based on articles originally printed in the magazine

Jerusalem Perspective, or on later essays published electronically at www.JerusalemPerspective.com. Many insights in these chapters are the product of discussion and collaboration with other members of the Jerusalem School of Synoptic Research, a think tank of scholars working to understand the Gospels in their historical Jewish context. Nonetheless, the conclusions put forward in this book are those of the author, rather than of the Jerusalem School as a whole.

Texts for Understanding Jesus

What are the documents that are most useful for understanding Jesus' ministry within its original setting? Enormous change occurred in Judaism in the four hundred years after the time of the Hebrew Scriptures, so the social context described in even its latest books is of limited value in understanding Jesus' time. However, Jesus peppered his teachings with references to Bible passages because his audience was highly literate regarding the Hebrew Bible, especially the Torah. Therefore, knowing these Scriptures and how they were interpreted in Jesus' time can be extremely helpful in understanding Jesus' words, even though they may not directly describe his world.

Documents from closer to the time of Jesus can provide more insight on his ministry's setting. The period between the Testaments was a time of great change, with the establishment of the synagogue and the rise of several sects within Judaism, including the Pharisees, Sadducees, and Essenes. None of these are mentioned in the Hebrew Scriptures, but understanding them is critical for a clear picture of Jesus' context. Historical works like Josephus can shed light on the political and social setting of Jesus' day. Jewish religious writings from the intertestamental period and from Jesus' time are important sources as well. These include books of the Apocrypha, particularly the Jewish Pseudepigrapha, that while not canonical, show the thinking of the intertestamental period. Also key are the Dead Sea Scrolls, an extensive library of writings and Scriptures from the Jewish Essene community who lived at Qumran between the third century B.C. and A.D. 68. These documents have revealed an enormous amount of new information on the religious thinking of Jesus' time, shedding light on the cultural conversation going on around Jesus.[2]

Additionally, collections of rabbinic teachings from two to five hundred years after his time can be very helpful for understanding Jesus' Jewish context. Although the time lag seems significant, a vast amount of religious literature of Jesus' time was memorized verbatim and transmitted orally from rabbi to student for hundreds of years, deliberately preserved only in oral form. This collection of scripture interpretation and legal codes was called the "Oral Torah," and was first recorded in a book called the Mishnah around A.D. 200.[3] Other collections of early rabbinic thought were written about that time as well, including the Tosephta, Sifre, Sifra, Mechilta, and the Beraitot.

The Mishnah includes much material on Jewish thought and practice from Jesus' time and even two hundred years preceding him. This collection is very valuable for understanding Jesus, because it is the product of the Pharisaic rabbis who commented on the same issues that Jesus did, and whose teaching was widely accepted by Jews of Jesus' day. In fact, Jesus' teaching shows more similarities to that of the Pharisees than any other sect of Judaism, although he was clearly distinct from them. His style was particularly similar to the Hasidim, charismatic rabbis that were close in theology to the Pharisees.[4]

A few hundred years after the Mishnah, a larger work was compiled called the Talmud, containing the Mishnah along with an expansive commentary on that work. One version known as the Jerusalem Talmud dates from approximately A.D. 400, and a much larger version, published in Babylon, dates from about 100 years later. The Babylonian Talmud is still central to Orthodox Judaism today. Although the sayings in the latter were not assembled until five hundred years after Jesus, they include many parables and sayings that were preserved orally from his day. With care as to the dating of material, all of these documents can be very useful for understanding the world in which Jesus lived.

A Closer Look at Jesus' Words

Another key to understanding Jesus' sayings is to look more closely at the peculiar style of language in which the Gospels preserved them. The Synoptic Gospels (Matthew, Mark and Luke) were written in Koine Greek that is elegant and polished in some places, but in other places awkward, the wording somewhat unnatural for Greek. This is because they reflect underlying Semitic idioms and sentence style that have been very literally translated into Greek. This style is found throughout the Synoptic Gospels and in the first half of the book of Acts, but not in John or elsewhere.

An important aspect of the underlying Semitic phrases is that they reflect Jesus' use of the idioms and technical terminology of other rabbis of his day. For example, Jesus frequently talked about the "kingdom of heaven." The Greek phrase *he basileia ton ouranon* is an extremely literal rendering of the Hebrew expression *malchut shamayim* (kingdom of heaven). In Hebrew, the word for "heaven" is plural, and is carefully preserved in the plural form of the Greek *ton ouranon*. The phrase "kingdom of heaven" and several other idioms found in the synoptic tradition are never found in the Hebrew Scriptures but were common terms among rabbis of Jesus' day, with specialized meanings and connotations that are not always obvious. Reading Jesus' words with an eye for their idiomatic Jewish language usage often gives new clarity to his sayings.

From the Semitic Greek that is found in the Synoptic Gospels scholars can gain additional insight by examining the nature of the sayings of Jesus synoptically — by comparing sayings between parallel gospel accounts. Often one Gospel has retained the Semitisms in a saying while another has translated it into more polished Greek, or included more explanation to clarify it to the Greek-speaking reader. Often the shorter, rougher passage retains Semitic nuances that throw light on the original idiomatic wording of the saying.[5]

Reconsidering Hebrew

Another key to understanding Jesus' words is to look more closely at the language in which he spoke. Jesus lived in a highly multilingual environment, with Hebrew, Aramaic and Greek likely spoken by most Jews of the time. The Gospels, at first glance, appear to indicate that Aramaic was the language of Jesus. It was the language of many inscriptions and place names, and along with Greek, was a language of official documents and trade.

Jesus certainly knew and spoke Aramaic when needed, but many scholars now believe that he did his teaching in Hebrew. The rabbis of Jesus' day and for hundreds of years after him delivered their parables, legal rulings, prayers and sermons entirely in Hebrew. In fact, there are several thousand parables and prayers recorded in rabbinic literature, and virtually all are in Hebrew, even when the surrounding text is in Aramaic.[6] This Hebrew was not the dialect of the Scriptures, but a newer, living language called Middle, or Mishnaic Hebrew. If Jesus functioned within Jewish society, he most likely delivered his teachings in Hebrew as well. Evidence for this comes from the fact that many Semitic idioms found in Jesus' stories and teachings translate well into Mishnaic Hebrew, but don't make sense in Aramaic at all.[7]

Because Hebrew and Aramaic are closely related languages, many of Jesus' words that appear to be Aramaic are actually found in Mishnaic Hebrew as well, including *abba* (father), *raka* (empty), *korban* (dedicated) and *rabboni* (my teacher or master). This explains why in John 20:16, the Greek text says that the word *rabboni* was Hebrew, although some scholars have thought that this was a mistaken reference to Aramaic.[8] To the contrary, Jews were very multilingual and well aware of the differences in the languages in use, as the following saying illustrates:

There are four languages which are fitting to be used by all. And they are: Greek for song, Latin for combat, Aramaic for dirges and Hebrew for conversation.[9]

Knowing that Jesus' teaching language was likely Mishnaic Hebrew greatly helps in reconstructing the words of Jesus, and aids in finding parallels in the teachings of other rabbis of that day which also were given in Hebrew.

Hebraic Idioms in the Gospels

Understanding that the language of Jesus' sayings was Hebrew leads to another observation, that many expressions in the Greek texts of the Synoptic Gospels seem to derive from Hebrew idioms. Every language has its own idioms which seem strange when translated literally out of their native setting, such as "hit the ceiling," "lose one's head," "be in hot water," or "kick the bucket."

The Hebrew language likewise has hundreds of idioms. For example: *taman et yado batsalahat*, literally, "buried his hand in the dish," means that someone idles away his time.

The Greek of the Gospels reflects many Hebraisms, such as "lift up the eyes and see," which appears in Luke 16:23 in a parable about a miserly rich man and a poor man named Lazarus. This same expression, *nasa et ha'eynayim vera'a*, had been current in Hebrew since biblical times, and appears thirty-five times in the Hebrew Scriptures. For instance, in the dramatic account of the first meeting of Isaac and his bride-to-be Rebekah, Isaac "lifted up his eyes and saw" the approaching Rebekah, and she "lifted up her eyes and saw" Isaac (Gen 24:63-64). There is no evidence of this expression being used in the normative Greek of Jesus' day, yet it is found in the Greek texts of the Synoptic Gospels. This idiom is also found in other Hebrew literature of the period.[10] It is important to realize that there may be Hebrew idioms preserved in the Greek of the Gospels. Just being aware of this can help us read English versions of the Gospels with more understanding.

Summary

All these observations about the Jewishness of Jesus, that he used rabbinic terminology and idioms, that his teachings were most likely in Hebrew, and that Jewish texts from near his time hold important clues for understanding him, are pivotal in the research of David Bivin and the insights that he shares in this book. The reader is invited to consider as well whether this approach does not shed much new light on the difficult words of Jesus.

---

[1] Tikva Frymer-Kensky, et al, eds, *Christianity in Jewish Terms*, (Boulder, CO: Westview Press, 2000), p. 96; Marvin Wilson, *Our Father Abraham*, (Grand Rapids, MI: Eerdmans, 1989), pp. 127–128.

[2] Examples of the usefulness of both intertestamental literature and the writings of the Essenes are presented later in this book. Refer to pp. 23–25 to see the concept of a "yoke" in earlier Jewish writings. See pp. 89–92 for how Essene writings help in understanding the context of Jesus' words to "love your enemies."

[3] For more on the Oral Torah, see pp. 41–42; regarding oral transmission and its accuracy in preserving literature, see pp. 33–34.

[4] Shmuel Safrai, "Jesus and the Hasidim," *Jerusalem Perspective* 42, 43 & 44 (Jan–Jun 1994), pp. 3–22.

[5] For more on exploring Semitisms and the synoptic relationship of the Gospels, see Robert Lindsey, "Four Keys for Better Understanding Jesus," *Jerusalem Perspective* 49 (Oct–Dec 1995), pp. 10–17, 38.

[6] See Shmuel Safrai, "Literary Languages in the Time of Jesus," *Jerusalem Perspective* 31 (Mar/Apr 1991), pp. 3–8.

[7] Randall Buth, "The Language of Jesus' Teaching" (subsection of "Aramaic Language"), *Dictionary of New Testament Background*, Craig Evans and Stanley Porter, eds. (Downers Grove, IL: Intervarsity, 2000), pp. 86–91.

[8] Buth, p. 89. Even though the Greek text of the New Testament refers to the language spoken as being Hebrew (Jn 5:2, 19:13, 17, 20; 20:16; Acts 21:40, 22:2; 26:14, Rev. 9:11; 16:16), some translators are so convinced that this is an error that they translate the Greek word *hebra'is* into English as "Aramaic." This is true in the New International Version, which often adds an explanatory note. See David Bivin, "The New International Jesus," *Jerusalem Perspective* 56 (Jul–Sep 1999), pp. 20–24.

[9] J. Megilla 71b, quoted by Safrai, p. 5. At the beginning of the 20th century, many scholars thought that the Hebrew of the Mishnah was an artificial language only used in rabbinic debate. The discovery of the Dead Sea Scrolls caused this hypothesis to be discarded. According to Michael Wise and Martin Abegg, "Prior to the discovery of the Dead Sea Scrolls, the dominant view of the Semitic languages of the period was as follows: Hebrew had died ... the spoken language of the Jews had in fact become Aramaic.... The discovery of the scrolls swept these linguistic notions into the trash bin." *The Dead Sea Scrolls, A New Translation* (San Francisco, CA: HarperCollins, 1999), pp. 8–9.

[10] E.g., m. Ta'anit 4:8. See David Bivin, "Hebraic Idioms in the Gospels," *Jerusalem Perspective* 22 (Sep/Oct 1989), pp. 6–7.

I.
A Jewish Rabbi
Named Jesus

1.

Jesus' Formal Education

The popular view of Jesus is that he was a simple, uneducated character from the provinces. But a careful reading of the New Testament suggests that Jesus was a scholar learned in the Scriptures and religious literature of the period, which was vast. The misunderstanding is due in part to a number of disparaging statements made about Nazareth and the Galilee such as, "Nazareth! Can anything good come from there?" (Jn 1:46), and "Utterly amazed, they asked: 'Are not all these men who are speaking Galileans?'" (Acts 2:7).

These statements may reflect a Judean bias against Galileans because some Judeans may have seen themselves as cultured and cosmopolitan. To them, the Galileans were provincials whose accent seemed coarse and unrefined. Actually, however, the reverse may have been true: the Galileans were more exposed to the outside world while the Judeans, living in the interior of the land, were partially sheltered from contact with foreign nations. The Galilee also was more urban, with many developed villages, while Judea was generally more rural in character. No doubt this same disdain toward Galileans prompted the assumption, preserved in John 7:15, that Jesus had no education: "The Jews [or, Judeans, also possible from the Greek] were amazed and asked, 'How did this man get such learning without having studied?'"

Such passages have given rise to the idea that Jesus and his disciples were uneducated simply because they came from Galilee. Surprisingly, however, the standard of education and religious training in Galilee surpassed that of Judea. Not only does the number of first-century Galilean rabbis exceed the number of Judean rabbis,[1] but the moral and ethical quality of their teaching is still considered more highly than that of their Judean counterparts. Such first-century Galilean sages as Yohanan ben Zakkai, Hanina ben Dosa, Abba Yose Holikofri of Tiv'on, Zadok and Jesus of Nazareth helped impart a deep understanding of the Torah to the residents of Galilee.

In addition to their high level of knowledge of and reverence for Scripture, the Galileans could be seen as the religious conservatives of the period. Jewish messianic nationalism flourished in the Galilee. Judah the Galilean, for example, was the founder of the "Zealots" movement, and it was in Galilee, not Judea, that the great revolt against Rome broke out in A.D. 66.

Jesus' Early Training

The New Testament says almost nothing about Jesus' life from after his birth until he appeared in the Temple at age twelve, and from then until he began his public ministry at about the age of thirty. But, the education and stages of life of a typical Jewish man in Jesus' day are described in the following rabbinic saying:

> At five years of age, the study of Scripture [Written Torah];
> At ten, the study of Mishnah [Oral Torah – the rabbinic commentary on the Written Torah];
> At thirteen, subject to the commandments [*Bar Mitzvah*, the religious coming-of-age ceremony];
> At fifteen, the study of Talmud [*halachot*, rabbinic legal decisions];
> At eighteen, the bridal canopy;
> At twenty, for pursuit [of livelihood];
> At thirty, the peak of strength...[2]

Although this statement cannot be dated with certainty, and may come from some one hundred years after the time of Jesus, there are many other passages in rabbinic works that indicate the importance placed upon the education of children and provide some insight into how the young Jesus was probably spending his time. Certainly education was highly valued in Jewish society.[3] The Talmud even suggests the preferred class size.[4]

A synagogue in the first century usually had its own *bet sefer* (elementary school) and *bet midrash* (secondary school) in which children and adults studied Torah and the oral traditions. Formal

Remains of the fourth-century synagogue at Capernaum

education ended at the age of twelve or thirteen when most children went to work. The more gifted students who so desired could continue their studies at the *bet midrash* together with adults who studied in their spare time. A few of the most outstanding *bet midrash* students eventually left home to study with a famous rabbi, being encouraged and sometimes supported by their families. Only the very promising students were urged to continue studying since their assistance was usually needed in agricultural work at home.[5]

One might assume that the synagogue, as the place of worship, would be considered more important or more sacred than the schools, but this was not the case. To this day the *bet midrash* is given more prominence than the synagogue — not because education is valued more highly than worship, but because Judaism does not make a distinction between the two. Indeed, Judaism has always held that study of Torah is one of the highest forms of worship.[6]

Learning Through Memorization

Although scrolls were used for reading and study, and the

practice of writing was highly developed, written material was expensive because all manuscripts had to be hand-copied by trained scribes. Scrolls, therefore, were relatively scarce, and even though in Jesus' time every Jewish home probably had at least one of the approximately twenty biblical scrolls, few people had immediate access to more than a very small part of the entire library of sacred literature. Consequently, learning involved a great deal of memorization.[7] In the eyes of the rabbis, repetition was the key, as these passages illustrate:

> A person who repeats his lesson a hundred times is not to be compared with him who repeats it a hundred and one times.[8]

> If [the student] learns Torah and does not go over it again and again, he is like a man who sows without reaping.[9]

Many methods were used to assist the student in memorizing his lessons, and one passage in the Talmud[10] even describes in detail the mnemonic devices employed to teach small children the Hebrew alphabet. Elementary school students, who studied seven days a week, were given no new material on the Sabbath, but rather used that time to memorize material learned earlier in the week.[11] Such memorization is still practiced today in the Middle East. One frequently can see young men walking back and forth along the roads at the outskirts of villages and towns, apparently talking to themselves. They actually are repeating and memorizing their lessons.

Memorization of Written Torah and of the Oral Torah was such a large part of Jewish education that most of them had large portions of the Scriptures and Oral Torah firmly committed to memory. From quite early in the Second Temple period, one could hardly find a little boy in the street who didn't know the Scriptures. According to Jerome (A.D. 342–420), who lived in Bethlehem and learned Hebrew from local Jewish residents in order to translate the Scriptures into Latin [producing the Vulgate Bible]: "There doesn't exist any Jewish child who doesn't know by heart the history from Adam to Zerubbabel [i.e., from the beginning to the end of the Bible]." Perhaps this was a bit of an exaggeration on Jerome's part, but in most cases his reports have proved reliable.[12]

From accounts found in Jewish sources such as those referred to above, one can form a reasonably accurate picture of what Jesus' childhood and adolescence were like. He was studying, memorizing large amounts of material – Scripture and commentary on Scripture – all the available sacred literature of the day. This was probably what most of the other Jewish boys of Jesus' day were doing as well.

---

[1] According to Shmuel Safrai, Professor of Jewish History of the Mishnaic and Talmudic Periods, Hebrew University.

[2] "... at forty, wisdom; at fifty, able to give counsel; at sixty, old age; at seventy, fullness of years; at eighty, the age of "strength"; at ninety, a bent body; at one hundred, as good as dead and completely passed from the world" (m. Avot 5:21).

[3] In his apology for Judaism, *Against Apion*, written to counter anti-Semitism, the first-century Jewish historian Josephus states, "Above all we pride ourselves on the education of our children, and regard as the most essential task in life the observance of our laws and of the pious practices based thereupon, which we have inherited." *Against Apion* 1:60 (Loeb ed.).

[4] "The maximum number of elementary pupils that should be placed under one teacher is twenty-five; if there are fifty, an additional teacher must be provided; if there are forty, a senior student should be engaged to assist the teacher" (b. Bava Batra 21a).

[5] Shmuel Safrai, "Education and the Study of Torah," in *The Jewish People in the First Century* (ed. Shmuel Safrai and Menahem Stern; Amsterdam: Van Gorcum, 1976), p. 953.

[6] See b. Shabbat 30a.

[7] Professor Safrai has written concerning educational methods of the period: "Individual and group study of the Bible, repetition of the passages, etc., were often done by chanting them aloud. There is the frequent expression, 'the chirping of children,' which was heard by people passing close by a synagogue as the children were reciting a verse. Adults too, in individual and group study, often read aloud; for it was frequently advised not to learn in a whisper, but aloud. This was the only way to overcome the danger of forgetting" (*The Jewish People in the First Century* p. 953).

[8] B. Hagigah 9b.

[9] B. Sanhedrin 99a.

[10] B. Shabbat 104a.

[11] Shmuel Safrai, "Education and the Study of Torah," (*The Jewish People in the First Century* p. 954).

[12] Shmuel Safrai, lecture on June 5, 1985.

"Jesus' Formal Education" was adapted and abridged from the article, "Jesus' Education," by David Bivin, which is available online at www.JerusalemPerspective.com.

2.

Following a Rabbi

Was Jesus a Rabbi?

By the time Jesus began his public ministry, he had not only received the thorough religious training typical of the average Jewish man of his day, he had probably spent years studying with one of the outstanding rabbis in the Galilee. Jesus thus appeared on the scene as a respected rabbi himself. Several passages in the Bible illustrate that he was recognized as such by his contemporaries:

> And Jesus answered and said to him, "Simon, I have something to say to you." And he said, "Rabbi, what is it?" (Lk 7:40)

> A lawyer asked him a question to test him: "Rabbi, what is the greatest commandment in the Torah?" (Mt 22:35-36)

> And behold, a [rich] man came up to him and said, "Rabbi, what good thing must I do to have eternal life?" (Mt 19:16)

> And someone in the crowd said to him, "Rabbi, order my brother to divide the inheritance with me." (Lk 12:13)

> And some of the Pharisees in the crowd said to him, "Rabbi, rebuke your disciples." (Lk 19:39)

> Some of the Sadducees came up to him...and they asked him, saying, "Rabbi...." (Lk 20:27-28)

The diversity of those who addressed Jesus as "rabbi" — a lawyer, a rich man, Pharisees, Sadducees and ordinary people — clearly underscore the point. To understand the full significance of Jesus being addressed "rabbi," one must know what a Jewish teacher of the first century was and how he functioned in that society.

The term "rabbi" is derived from the Hebrew word *rav*, which in biblical Hebrew meant "much, many, numerous, great." It also was sometimes used to refer to high government officials or army officers (e.g., Jer 39:3, 13). In Jesus' day, *rav* was used to refer to the master of a slave or of a disciple. Therefore *rabbi* literally meant "my master" and was a term of respect used by slaves in addressing their owners and by disciples in addressing their teachers.

It was only after A.D. 70 that "rabbi" became a formal title for a teacher[1] and thus cannot technically be applied to Jesus. A learned teacher of this time period is commonly referred to as a "sage," so that term is a very appropriate way to refer to Jesus. Nonetheless, the designation "rabbi" may still be more helpful than any other in conveying a correct image of Jesus to the average Christian reader, if it suggests that Jesus was recognized among the Jews of his day as a teacher of Scripture, and that he was famous enough to draw students to himself.

A Typical First-Century Jewish Rabbi

From the gospel accounts, Jesus clearly appears as a typical first-century sage, or Jewish teacher. He traveled from place to place; he depended upon the hospitality of the people; he taught outdoors, in homes, in villages, in synagogues and in the Temple; he had disciples who followed him as he traveled. This is the very image of a Jewish teacher in the land of Israel at that time.

Perhaps the most convincing proof that Jesus was a sage was his style of teaching, because he used the same methods of Scripture interpretation and instruction as other Jewish teachers of his day. A simple example of this is Jesus' use of parables to convey his teachings. Parables such as Jesus used were extremely prevalent among ancient Jewish sages, and over 4,000 of them have survived in rabbinic literature.

Jewish teachers of first-century Israel lacked the sophisticated methods of mass communication we have today. Consequently the rabbis of Jesus' day spent much of their time traveling throughout the country, much like the ancient prophets, to communicate their teachings and interpretations of Scripture. An itinerant rabbi was the norm rather than exception. Hundreds and perhaps thousands of such rabbis circulated in the land of Israel in the first century. These rabbis did not hesitate to travel to the smallest of villages or the most remote parts of the country. In some instances they would conduct their classes in someone's home, but often classes would be held in the village square or under a tree.

Jesus' ministry also followed this custom. Much of Jesus' teaching was done indoors: in homes (Lk 10:38–42), synagogues (Mt 4:23), even in the Temple (Mt 21:23; Lk 21:37). But we also find Jesus, like a typical first-century rabbi, teaching outside in impromptu situations. A picturesque account of Jesus teaching from a boat is found in Luke 5. The feeding of the five thousand occurred in "a lonely place" (Mt 14:13; Mk 6:32; Lk 9:12), and the Sermon on the Mount was so named because it was delivered in a rural location.

From the Gospels we learn that Jesus likewise moved from place to place a great deal, often accompanied by crowds. Mark 6:6, for example, records that Jesus "went around from village to village teaching." He traveled considerably in Galilee, especially in the vicinity of the Sea of Galilee, and likely in Judea as well.[2]

To Earn a Living

For all the traveling and teaching the rabbis did, rabbinic literature contains many prohibitions against charging a fee for teaching the Scriptures.[3] Because of these interdictions, almost all rabbis practiced a trade. Some were scribes, others sandal makers, leather workers or bakers. Jesus was a craftsman himself, according to Mark 6:3, and Acts 18:3 notes that Paul supported himself by making tents.[4]

Despite the fact that most rabbis had professions, they were not always able to support themselves as they traveled throughout the land. The traveling sage could not easily set up a shop due to the shortness of his stay in any given location. Nor would it have been fair when visiting smaller communities to take work away from a local resident in the same profession. Also, work could not readily be found for the large number of disciples who often accompanied a rabbi. Therefore the rabbi and his disciples were necessarily dependent upon the hospitality of the communities they visited.

A rabbi's stay in a community might last from a few days to weeks or months. Although rabbis would not accept payment for teaching Torah, most would accept lodging, and usually food as well, for themselves and their students. Jesus clearly felt that his disciples should be entirely supported by their hosts when out teaching. In one instance, he sent out disciples commanding them to take nothing with them, neither food nor money (Lk 10:4).

Covered in the Dust of the Rabbi

A saying from approximately one hundred years before Jesus supports this picture of the rabbi in the land of Israel, and is remarkably descriptive of the ministry of Jesus:

Let your home be a meeting-house for the sages, and cover yourself with the dust of their feet, and drink in their words thirstily.[5]

In the context of this statement, "a meeting-house for the sages" should be understood to mean a place where the rabbis could hold classes, not a place where they themselves could assemble. Had people not opened their homes to the rabbis, it would have been impossible for them to reach the masses with their message.

The story of Mary and Martha in Luke 10:38–42 offers a good example of a family who heeded this injunction to be hospitable to rabbis and their disciples. Not only did they make their home

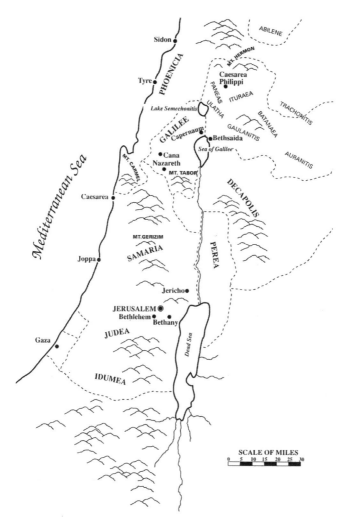

Israel at the time of Jesus

available as a meeting place for the rabbi Jesus, but Mary is described as "sitting at the feet" of the rabbi, and "drinking in his words thirstily."

The words "cover yourself with the dust of their feet" in the rabbinic quotation have traditionally been understood to mean, "to sit at the feet of a rabbi," to humbly learn from him, as Mary did.

- 13 -

However, these words might convey a different picture. For the long-term disciple, learning from a rabbi meant considerable traveling as well. One literally had to follow a rabbi to learn from him,[6] so if your rabbi traveled, you did too. To this day the unpaved roads of Israel are covered with a fine dust and as a result, when people walk along these roads they invariably raise a considerable cloud of dust. Any group of disciples following a rabbi would be covered with dust at the end of a journey, and if one wanted to travel with a rabbi, one literally had to cover oneself with the dust of his feet!

Making Disciples

The rabbis were sincerely interested in leading more and more people to "take upon themselves the yoke of Torah," a rabbinic expression for accepting God's reign over one's life, to live according to his will. To accomplish this, they trained advanced students as disciples, and they taught the masses. To "make many disciples" was one of the three earliest sayings recorded in the Mishnah,[7] and perhaps the highest calling of a rabbi. Often he would select and train large numbers of disciples, but he was perfectly willing to teach as few as two or three students. It is recorded that the Apostle Paul's teacher Gamaliel had one thousand disciples who studied with him.[8]

Jesus, too, had many permanent students. We know about Jesus' inner circle of twelve disciples who received special training, but these were not his only disciples. He called others to follow him, including Levi, a tax collector, who we read "left everything" to respond (Lk 5:28). In Matthew 8:19 we read of another man who was warned by Jesus of the price he would have to pay after he perhaps too quickly and easily blurted out, "Teacher, I will follow you wherever you go!" Two would-be disciples were rebuked by Jesus when they asked his permission to tend to important family responsibilities before answering his call (Lk 9:59–62). And Jesus also called a rich man, demanding that he divest himself of his wealth before becoming his disciple (Mk 10:21).

Luke 19:37 notes that near the end of Jesus' life, a "multitude" of his disciples accompanied him as he entered Jerusalem. We can gain an idea of the size of that "multitude" from the number of

Galilean disciples alone — one hundred twenty — who remained in Jerusalem after Jesus' crucifixion (Acts 1:15). Jesus' twelve disciples spent years of intense study and practical training with their master. Later, they themselves were sent out to make disciples and pass on Jesus' teaching.

---

[1] Emil Schürer (Vermes, Millar and Black, eds.), *The History of the Jewish People in the Age of Jesus Christ*, vol. 2, (Edinburgh: T & T Clark, 1973), pp. 325–326.

[2] David Bivin, "Jesus in Judea," *Jerusalem Perspective* 2 (Nov 1987), pp. 1–2.

[3] "He who makes a profit from the words of Torah has brought about his own destruction," (m. Avot 4:5); "Do not charge for teaching Torah. Accept no remuneration for it" (Derek Eretz Zuta 3:3).

[4] Or working leather, according to F. J. Foakes-Jackson and K. Lake, *The Acts of the Apostles*, vol. 4, (London: Macmillan, 1920–33) p. 223.

[5] M. Avot 1:4. Yose ben Yoezer, the author of this saying, lived in the first half of the second century B.C., and was one of the earliest of the sages of the Mishnah.
The interpretation of "being covered in dust" as walking along behind a traveling rabbi, rather than sitting at his feet, is from Prof. Shmuel Safrai.

[6] Ibid.

[7] M. Avot 1:1.

[8] B. Sotah 49b.

"Following a Rabbi" was adapted from the following articles by David Bivin, available at www.JerusalemPerspective.com: "The Traveling Rabbi," "At the Feet of a Rabbi," and "Was Jesus a Rabbi?"

3.

First-Century Discipleship

The call to be a rabbi's disciple in first-century Israel often meant leaving relatives and friends and traveling the country under austere conditions. It also meant total commitment. A prospective disciple first had to be sure his priorities were in order. Consider the words of the man who said to Jesus, "I will follow you, Lord, but first let me go back and say good-bye to my family" (Lk 9:61). Jesus' reply shows that only those who were prepared to commit themselves totally to him would be welcome: "No one who puts his hand to the plow and then looks back is fit for the kingdom of God" (Lk 9:62). This is emphasized in Jesus' response to another man who offered to follow him, but only after burying his father. "Let the dead bury their dead," Jesus told him (Lk 9:60; Mt 8:22).

Apparently, Jesus' replies were directed towards persons whom he had invited to leave home and serve a full-time apprenticeship with him. This form of discipleship was a unique feature of ancient Jewish society.

Sacrifice

According to one rabbinic saying, there are certain things such as honoring one's father and mother of which a person "benefits from the interest" in this world, while "the principal" remains for him in the world to come.[1] "But," the passage goes on, "the study of Torah is equal to them all." Jesus said something similar: As important as it is to honor one's parents, leaving home to study Torah with him was even more important.

To the rich man mentioned in Luke 18, the call to follow Jesus meant giving up all his wealth. The price was too high for him and he did not become one of Jesus' disciples. Peter reminded Jesus that he and the others who had accepted Jesus' call were different: "We have left everything to follow you." "Amen!" said Jesus — in other words, "Yes, you have done that and it is commendable." Jesus went on to promise that anyone who had made the sacrifice of total commitment for the sake of the Kingdom of God would receive something of much greater value than what he had given up, and eternal life in the world to come (Lk 18:28-30).

Commitment

Jesus did not want his prospective disciples to have any false expectations, so he frequently stressed the need to count the cost before making a commitment to him:

> Which of you, if he wanted to build a tower, would not first sit down and estimate the cost to see if he had enough money to complete it? ... Likewise, any of you who is not ready to leave all his possessions cannot be my disciple. (Lk 14:28-33)

Jesus was very clear about the degree of commitment that was required of a disciple:

> If anyone comes to me and does not hate his father, mother, wife, children, brothers, sisters, and himself as well, he cannot be my disciple. Whoever does not bear his cross and follow me cannot be my disciple. (Lk 14:26-27)

In this context the word "hate" does not carry the meaning it normally has in English usage, but seems to be used in a Hebraic sense. In Hebrew "hate" can also mean "love less" or "put in second place." For example, Genesis 29:31 states that Leah was "hated," but the context indicates that Leah was not unloved but rather loved less than Jacob's other wife Rachel. Note that the preceding verse specifically says that Jacob loved Rachel more than Leah.

A second illustration of this particular Hebraic shade of meaning of the word "hate" is found in Deuteronomy 21:15: "If a man has two wives, one loved and the other hated...." Here too, the context shows that the "hated" wife is only second in affection and not really hated in the English sense of the word. Likewise in Jesus' statement, he was saying that whoever did not love him more than his own family or even his own self could not be his disciple.

Jesus also alluded to the rigors of the itinerant life of a rabbi when he said, "Foxes have holes and birds of the air have nests, but the Son of Man has nowhere to lay his head" (Lk 9:57–58). The burden Jesus' disciples had to bear was a heavy one, but it was similar to what other first-century sages demanded of their disciples and would not have been considered extreme by the standards of first-century Jewish society.

Another hardship a disciple could face was being away from his wife. Disciples commonly were single, but since marriage took place at a relatively early age, usually by eighteen,[2] many disciples had a wife and children. For example, the mother-in-law of one of Jesus' disciples, Peter, is mentioned in Luke 4:38. If married, a man needed the permission of his wife to leave home for longer than thirty days to study with a sage.[3]

The call of Elisha to become Elijah's disciple (1 Kings 19:19–21)

Like a Father

Despite the many hardships, there was nothing to compare with the exhilaration of following and learning from a great rabbi and being in the circle of his disciples. A special relationship developed between rabbi and disciple in which the rabbi became like a father. In fact he was more than a father and was to be honored above the disciple's own father, as this passage from the Mishnah indicates:

When one is searching for the lost property both of his father and of his teacher, his teacher's loss takes precedence over that of his father since his father brought him only into the life of this world, whereas his teacher, who taught him wisdom [i.e., Torah], has brought him into the life of the World to Come. But if his father is no less a scholar than his teacher, then his father's loss takes precedence.... If his father and his teacher are in captivity, he must first ransom his teacher, and only afterwards his father — unless his father is himself a scholar and then he must first ransom his father.[4]

If it seems shocking that someone would ransom his teacher before his own father, it is only because we do not understand the tremendous love and respect that disciples, and the community at large, had for their rabbis. Disciples were often even referred to as rabbi's "sons," a tradition from the time of Elijah.[5]

Similarly, it may seem cruel that Jesus would not allow a prospective disciple to say good-bye to his family before setting out to follow him. However, it would have seemed quite reasonable and normal to Jesus' first-century contemporaries. It would have been perfectly clear to them what Jesus meant when he said, "No one can be my disciple who does not hate his father and mother, wife and children, brothers and sisters" (Lk 14:26).

---

[1] M. Peah 1:1.

[2] M. Avot 5:21.

[3] M. Ketubot 5:6.

[4] M. Bava Metsi'a 2:11.

[5] The ancient prophets of Israel like Elijah and Elisha traveled with bands of followers called the "sons of the prophets" (e.g., 2 Kings 2:3, 5, 7, 15). These were not their physical sons, but rather their disciples.

The father-son relationship could be seen in Elijah and Elisha. Elisha called out to Elijah as "my father" at his departure (2 Kings 2:12), and asked to receive a double inheritance like that of a first-born son (2 Kings 2:9), suggesting a close father-son-like bond between the two that was likely a model for later rabbi-disciple relationships.

The use of "son" as a synonym for "disciple" still persisted in

Hebrew during the time of Jesus, as illustrated by this example:

> If I cast out demons by [the power of] Beelzebul, by [the power of] whom do your sons cast them out? (Lk 11:19)

This may also be behind Paul's reference to his disciple Timothy as "my beloved son" (2 Tim 1:2).

"First-Century Discipleship" was adapted and abridged from the article, "First-century Discipleship," by David Bivin, which is available online at www.JerusalemPerspective.com.

4.

Taking on Jesus' Yoke

Come to me, all you who are weary and burdened, and I will give you rest. Take my yoke upon you and learn from me, for I am gentle and humble in heart, and you will find rest for your souls. For my yoke is easy and my burden is light. (Mt 11:28-30; NIV)

How would Jesus' first listeners have heard his words about taking on his yoke? Learning what a "yoke" meant in the writings and culture of Jesus' time will greatly clarify his words. In a rabbi-disciple relationship, the disciple was expected to place himself in a position of total obedience and dedication to his rabbi and his philosophy. It was his desire to become just like him. This was said to be taking on the "yoke" of the rabbi.

Certainly the impression of a "yoke" (of oxen for example) comes immediately to mind as burdensome. But in the proper context, taking on a rabbi's yoke was not negative. When one's desire is to pull the same load as his teacher, the best way to do it is to willingly bind oneself to his yoke and cart.

Keys to Understanding Jesus' Words

Although extraordinarily beautiful, Jesus' saying is difficult to understand. What is this meaning of this saying, and what was Jesus' "yoke" and "burden"? The setting for Matthew 11:28-30 is not easy to establish, but in spite of this, passages from Jewish literature may help us determine Jesus' intent. In Ben Sira (also known as "Ecclesiasticus,") a Greek book of the Apocrypha that predated Jesus by over one hundred years, there exists an astounding parallel to Jesus' words:

Draw near to me, you unlearned, and lodge in the house

of study. Why are you slow, and what do you say about these things, your souls being very thirsty? I opened my mouth and said, "Buy her [wisdom] for yourselves without money. Put your neck under [her] yoke, and let your soul receive instruction. She is to be found nearby. See with your eyes how, with only a little labor, I have gotten much rest." (Ben Sira 51:23–27)

The Ben Sira passage contains the same themes found in Matthew 11:28–30:

- Drawing near to a source of instruction
- Taking up of a yoke or burden
- The labor of learning that results in finding rest

Ben Sira 51:27 implies that "the yoke is easy" (Mt 11:30) and the words "let your soul receive instruction" are similar to Jesus' saying to "learn from me." Key words found in the two passages include: "find/found," "your souls," "yoke" and "burden." Similar themes are seen in a second passage, which adds to our understanding of Jesus' saying:

Listen, my son, and accept my judgment; do not reject my counsel. Put your feet into her fetters, and your neck into her collar. Put your shoulder under her and carry her, and do not fret under her bonds. Come to her with all your soul, and keep her ways with all your might. Search out and seek, and she will become known to you; and when you get hold of her, do not let her go. For at last you will find the rest she gives, and she will be changed into joy for you. Then her fetters will become for you a strong protection, and her collar a glorious robe. Her yoke is a golden ornament, and her bonds are a cord of blue. You will wear her like a glorious robe, and put her on like a crown of gladness. (Ben Sira 6:23–31)

This passage also has much in common with Matthew 11:28–30. "Come to her with all your soul" reminds us of Jesus' "Come to me." "You will find the rest she gives" is echoed by Jesus (Mt 11:29). "Her yoke...and her bonds" is paralleled by Jesus' "my yoke...my burden." According to Ben Sira, wisdom's yoke, that is, the burden of study, will become joy, strong protection, a golden ornament, a cord of blue, a glorious robe and a crown of gladness. In other words, although the yoke is a burden, the bearer will experience it as easy and light. Probably, like the passages above, Matthew 11:28–30 refers to a context of learning. This suggests that Jesus was likely not contrasting his burden to the heavy burdens of the Pharisees to which he referred elsewhere (Mt 23:4), but rather, as he extended an invitation to prospective students to join his band of traveling students, he was alluding to the burden, or cost, of discipleship.

The Cost of Discipleship

The life of a disciple was not a bed of roses. In the Mishnah it is referred to as "a painful existence": "This is the way [to acquire knowledge] of the Torah: eat bread with salt, drink water by measure [Ezek 4:11], sleep on the ground, live a painful existence [literally, life of sorrow], and labor [studying] the Torah."[1]

Like other rabbis of his day, Jesus clearly indicated that a disciple's existence would be difficult: "Foxes have holes and birds of the air have nests, but the Son of Man has no place to lay his head" (Lk 9:58). In other words, his disciples would lead an itinerant lifestyle without permanent accommodations. The life of a student engaged in study with him would be rigorous and great sacrifice would be required. Such a lifestyle would necessarily be characterized by extreme dedication to the task and to the teacher.

In this teaching, Jesus extended a call to prospective disciples. As these pupils well knew, the study of Torah was a yoke, a heavy burden. "But," said Jesus, "my yoke is easy," that is, "studying with me will be so exhilarating that you won't even notice the yoke's weight." One can be invigorated by a heavy workload when the work is interesting. On the other hand, boredom and frustration can make even the smallest amount of work exhausting.

On the one hand, Jesus advised students who considered joining his disciples to consider very carefully the price they would have to pay. He gave two illustrations to make his point, likening it to the weighty decision to spend resources to build a tower or to go to war (Lk 14:26–27; 28–33). But on the other hand, Jesus promised students that they would be more than compensated for whatever sacrifices they were required to make ("the yoke would be easy"). When Peter exclaimed, "Look, we have left our possessions (or, our families) to follow you" (Lk 18:28), Jesus responded, "No one has left house [that is, family]...for the sake of the Kingdom of Heaven [that is, Jesus' disciples] who will not receive much more in this life" (Lk 18:29–30).

In other words, the joy and satisfaction that a student of Jesus received far outweighed the sacrifices that he was required to make. He taught that the value of being part of the Kingdom of Heaven was inestimable; it was like the value of buried treasure or a priceless fine pearl (Mt 13:44–46).

Not the Burden of the Commandments

In attempting to understand the meaning of "burden" (Greek: *phortion*) of which Jesus here speaks, one cannot ignore his use of "heavy burdens" (*phortia barea*) in Matthew 23:4, nor the use of "burden" (Greek: *baros*, "burden, load, weight") in a letter sent from the apostles and elders of Jerusalem to the Gentile believers in Antioch, Syria and Cilicia (Acts 15:28).[2]

> The scribes and the Pharisees sit on Moses' seat; so practice and observe whatever they tell you, but not what they do; for they preach, but do not practice. They bind heavy burdens, hard to bear, and lay them on men's shoulders; but they themselves will not move them with their finger. (Mt 23:2–4; RSV)

This basalt "Seat of Moses" was found in the synagogue at Chorazin.

Jesus stated that the scribes and Pharisees bound "heavy burdens" and placed them on people's shoulders. These burdens were the Pharisees' religious rulings, the commandments of the Oral Torah, as confirmed by the word "bind," a Hebraism for "to give a *halachic* prohibition."[3]

In contrast to most authorities, I assume that the "burden" of Matthew 11:30 did not refer to the burden of keeping the Pharisees' oral commandments,[4] but to the heavy burden that disciple was required to bear in order to gain a thorough knowledge of Torah. The word "bind" and the plural "burdens" in Matthew 23:24 help to confirm this assumption.

Obviously, Jesus did not think that observance of the Torah's commandments — oral as well as written — was unimportant.[5] After all, it was he who said, "Practice and observe whatever they [the Pharisees] tell you" (Mt 23:3). He was confident that thorough study and proper understanding of the Torah would result in observance of its commandments.

The Temple Mount from the south, as it would have looked in Jesus' day

Allusions to Other Scriptures

Come to me, all you who are weary and burdened, and I

will give you rest. Take my yoke upon you and learn from me, for I am gentle and humble in heart, and you will find rest for your souls. For my yoke is easy and my burden is light. (Mt 11:28–30; NIV)

Come to me... Likely, an invitation to learn from Jesus, to become his disciple.[6] According to Ben Sira it was Wisdom who invited people to come to her, find rest and accept her yoke.

...you who are weary and burdened. Jesus' words may reflect Jeremiah 31:25: "I will give drink to the weary and fill the faint."[7] The Septuagint's rendering of this verse (= Jer 38:25) is: "I gave drink to every thirsty soul and filled every hungry soul."

...and I will give you rest. Here, Jesus may have inserted a messianic claim: The Messiah was expected to bring rest for the righteous.[8] More startlingly, Jesus alluded to Exodus 33:14: "The LORD replied, 'My Presence will go with you, and I will give you rest [*va-hanihoti lach*]'" (NIV).[9] By using the words, "and I will give you rest," Jesus spoke in a way that only God speaks.[10] (See discussion below.)

Take my yoke upon you... The command "Take" is synonymous with "Come" in the preceding sentence (vs. 28). "Yoke" probably referred to the hardships connected with advanced study of Torah and the rigors of being a disciple (at that time, a full-time disciple of a sage was roughly the equivalent of the post-doctoral student of today). "Yoke" also could have been a reference to obedience to the commandments of the Torah,[11] or to Jesus' interpretation of them.[12]

...and learn from me, for I am gentle (meek) and humble in heart. We should notice that the Greek does not read, "learn of me," but, "learn from me," perhaps meaning, once again, "Come, study in my traveling school."[13]

One should compare Jesus' self-characterization, "meek and humble," with the description of Moses: "Now Moses was a very humble man, more so than any other man on earth" (Num 12:3; JPS). Perhaps Jesus was hinting that he was the "prophet like Moses" prophesied in Deuteronomy 18:15, 18.[14]

...you will find rest for your souls. An obvious allusion to Jeremiah 6:16: "This is what the LORD says: 'Stand at the crossroads and

look; ask for the ancient paths, ask where the good way is, and walk in it, and you will find rest for your souls.' But you said, 'We will not walk in it'" (NIV). Here, too, by using "and you will find rest for your souls," Jesus could have been speaking as only God speaks.

...*my yoke is easy and my burden is light.* The Greek adjective *chrestos* (easy) appears in the New Testament only here, in Luke 6:35 and 1 Peter 2:3; the Greek adjective *elaphron* [light; insignificant] only here and in 2 Corinthians 4:17. The two words appear in a passage that is full of Hebrew parallelism and translates easily to Hebrew.

Allusions with Powerful Implications

It is important to note that if when Jesus said, "Take my yoke upon you," he spoke of the keeping of commandments, Jesus might have been speaking as only God speaks. By calling this yoke "my yoke" (and the burden "my burden"), Jesus could have been making a shocking statement. The keeping of commandments was referred to as a "yoke," but it is unlikely that a rabbi would have made the claim that this yoke was "his."

Jesus made abundant messianic statements. By alluding to Scripture, he claimed to be the "Son of Man" of Daniel 7:13 (Lk 22:69,[15] 19:10; Mt 25:31); the "Green Tree" of Ezekiel 20:47 (Lk 23:31); the "King" (Mt 25:34); "Lord of the Sabbath" (Mt 12:8; Lk 6:5); and "greater than Jonah and Solomon" (Lk 11:31–32). By others, Jesus was referred to by such messianic titles as "Lord" (Lk 5:8); "Son of God" (Lk 1:35); "Son of David" (Lk 18:38); and the "Prophet Like Moses,"[16] the Last Redeemer of Deuteronomy 18:15 (Lk 7:16).

However, an audacious claim was almost never Jesus' main thrust. Into his teaching, which addressed specific situations and a wide variety of general subjects, he inserted, naturally and almost unconsciously, very subtle allusions to Scriptures that had been interpreted messianically by contemporary teachers and their predecessors.

Some of Jesus' allusions seem to be more than "mere" messianic claims. In delivering his teaching, apparently he sometimes spoke as only God speaks. For instance, in the preface to his *Parable of the House Built on Solid Foundations*, Jesus said,

"Everyone who hears these words of mine and does [i.e., keeps, observes] them will be like a wise man..." (Mt 7:24; Lk 6:47), employing "my words" when he spoke of hearing and doing God's commandments. Likewise, he proclaimed, "I will build my community [congregation, assembly]..." (Mt 16:18). Jesus' "my yoke" (= "my burden") in Matthew 11:29-30 should be compared to his "my words" and "my community." Jesus also spoke like God when he said, "The Son of Man has come to seek and to save the lost" (Lk 19:10), a clear reference to Ezekiel 34 where it is God who says repeatedly that he will seek and save his lost sheep. By claiming to be the "Seeker and Saver of the Lost," Jesus assumed a function of God, that of being the "Shepherd of the Lost Sheep."

---

[1] M. Avot 6:4.

[2] One also might consider 1 John 5:3: "This is love for God: to obey his commands. And his commands are not burdensome [bareiai]" (NIV), since in this verse we have a Greek adjective for "heavy, burdensome" in reference to God's commandments. However, it is possible that the writer of 1 John was influenced by Matthew 11:28–30, Matthew 23:4, and perhaps also by Acts 15.

[3] "Bind" and its opposite, "loose," are rabbinic idioms for "prohibit" and "permit" in reference to legal rulings. See pp. 98–100.

[4] Most commentators express an extreme bias against the Pharisees and the Oral Torah. Weiss writes: "Jesus indignantly describes the rules the Pharisaic rabbis lay on the righteous as...'heavy burdens that cannot be borne,' Mt. 23:4...The real concerns of the Law...are overwhelmed by casuistic and ritualistic obligations, i.e., by these *phortia* [burdens]. This helps us to understand the Saviour's call...in which Jesus promises refreshment to the weary and heavy-laden if they accept His *phortion* [burden], Mt. 11:28–30" (Konrad Weiss, "*Phortion*," *Theological Dictionary of the New Testament*, Vol. 9 (1974), G. Kittel, et al, ed. [Grand Rapids, MI: Eerdmans, 1964–1976] p. 85). Albright and Mann opine: "An easy yoke and a light burden are offered in exchange for the arbitrary demands of Pharisaic legalism and the uncertainties of ever-proliferating case law" (W. F. Albright and C. S. Mann, *Matthew* [Anchor Bible vol. 26; Garden City: Doubleday, 1971], p. 146). Robert H. Gundry writes: "...the burden Jesus puts on his disciples in chap. 11 contrasts with the burdens the scribes and Pharisees put on their followers in chap. 23. Confirmation that Matthew intends his readers to relate the two passages in this way comes from his omitting 'your burden' in 23:4 (again cf. Lk 11:46)" (*Matthew: A Commentary on His Handbook for a*

Mixed Church under Persecution, [2nd ed.; Grand Rapids, MI: Eerdmans, 1994] p. 219). Donald A. Hagner speaks of "the burdensome and tiring way of the Pharisees" (*Matthew*, p. 325), and "the overwhelming nomism of the Pharisees," stating that their rulings "involved a complicated casuistry" (p. 323). In his view, the Pharisees were Jesus' "primary rivals" (p. 324). For a more accurate appraisal of the Pharisees and their teaching, see David Flusser, *Jesus* (3rd ed.; Jerusalem: Magnes, 2001), pp. 66–73, 89, 150, 182–3, 202–3.

[5] Nor was Jesus suggesting, in Matthew 11:28–30, new, lighter commandments as replacements for the commandments of the Torah. He would never have contrasted his commandments with God's commandments: Until the end of time, not the smallest letter of God's Torah will ever pass away from the Torah, he said (Mt 5:18) (see pp. 94–96). Furthermore, Jesus himself observed the commandments, even commandments of the Oral Torah. For more on Jesus' observance of Jewish laws of his time, see pp. 41–46, 49–52, and 55–57. For the early church's ruling on Gentile observance of the commandments, see pp. 141–44.

[6] According to Hagner, "The invitation to come to Jesus is an invitation to discipleship, that is, to follow him and his teaching. 'Yoke' *(dzugon)* is a common metaphor for the law, both in Judaism (m. Avot 3:5; m. Berachot 2:2; cf. 1QH 6:19) and in the NT (Acts 15:10; Gal 5:1)." (*Matthew* [Word Bible Commentary 33A–33B; Dallas: Word Books, 1993–1995], p. 324). See also Sir 6:26, 28, 30 [Hebrew]; 24:19; 51:26.

[7] Gundry writes: "'Who are weary and burdened' in vs. 28a echoes Jer 31:25: 'for I have satisfied the weary [LXX: thirsty] soul, and every faint [LXX: hungry] soul I have replenished.' 'And I will give you refreshment' in verse 28b echoes the very same words in Exod 33:14. 'And you will find refreshment for your souls' in verse 29d is a verbatim quotation of Jer 6:16" (*Matthew*, p. 219).

[8] Samuel Tobias Lachs points out that "one of the blessings forthcoming in the messianic age will be the giving of rest to the weary pious" (*A Rabbinic Commentary on the New Testament: The Gospels of Matthew, Mark, and Luke* [Hoboken, NJ: Ktav, 1987], p. 196). Lachs cites En. 48.4, Pesiq. Rab Kah. 27 (163a), and Pesiq. Rab. 32 (149a) in support of his statement (p. 196, n. 1).

[9] The sense of *va-hanihoti lach* is probably not "and I will give you rest" in the absolute sense, that is, total or complete rest, but as the JPS renders, "I will lighten your burden."

[10] W. D. Davies and Dale C. Allison, Jr., imply that "and I will give you rest" did not come originally from the mouth of Jesus, but is a quotation from Exod 33:14 that was inserted by a later editor: "The closest OT parallel to Jesus' words, "and I will give you rest,' is Exod 33:14, where God says to Moses: 'and I will give you rest'...Note that whereas in the

OT text it is God, not Moses, who gives rest, in the NT Jesus gives it. Once more, then, Jesus is greater than Moses" (*A Critical and Exegetical Commentary on the Gospel According to Saint Matthew* International Critical Commentary, vol. 2, [Edinburgh: T&T Clark, 1988–1997], p. 287).

[11] F. J. Foakes Jackson and Kirsopp Lake, commenting on the use of "yoke" in Acts 15:10, state: "*Zygon ('ol)* was commonly used by Jewish writers in the sense of 'obligation'" (*The Acts of the Apostles,* vol. 4 [London: Macmillan, 1920–33], pp. 173–74). Davies and Allison remark: "The word [yoke] came to be a metaphor for obedience, subordination, servitude" (*A Critical and Exegetical Commentary on the Gospel According to Saint Matthew*, vol. 2, p. 289). According to Gundry (citing Acts 15:10; Gal 5:1; Sir 51:26; Pss. Sol. 7:9; 19:32; m. Avot 3:6; 2 Apoc. Bar. 41:3; and b. Berachot 13a), "yoke" is a well-known metaphor for obedience (*Matthew: A Commentary on His Handbook for a Mixed Church under Persecution*, p. 219). Weiss comments: "In rabbinic texts, *masa'* [burden]...has...the transfigurative sense of 'obligation,' 'duty' (j. Ber. 3, 1 [5d, 53–56. 61])" (*"Phortion,"* Theological Dictionary of the New Testament, vol. 9, p. 85).

[12] In Hagner's opinion, "When Jesus invites people with the words... 'take my yoke upon you,' he invites them to follow his own teaching as the definitive interpretation of the law... The same point is stressed in the next clause...'learn from me'" (*Matthew*, p. 324).

[13] For the Greek verb *manthanein* (to study) with the preposition *apo* (from), see Matthew 24:32 (= Mk 13:28) and Josephus Antiq. 8:317 ("He [Ahab] learned from her [Jezebel] to worship her native gods").

[14] The NIV's rendering of *prays* in Matthew 11:29 is "gentle." But *prays* is the Septuagint's usually translation of *anav* (meek), so Jesus might have used the same Hebrew word, *anav*, that described Moses. *Prays* is also the Septuagint's translation of *ani* (humble), for instance, in Zech 9:9: "Rejoice greatly, Fair Zion; Raise a shout, Fair Jerusalem! Lo, your king is coming to you. He is victorious, triumphant, Yet humble, riding on an ass, On a donkey foaled by a she-ass" (JPS).

[15] See Randall Buth, "Jesus' Most Important Title," *Jerusalem Perspective* 25 (Mar/Apr 1990), pp. 11–15.

[16] David Bivin, "'Prophet' as a Messianic Title" *Jerusalem Perspective* 2 (Nov 1987), pp. 3–4. Also see pp. 133–35.

"Taking on Jesus' Yoke" was adapted and abridged from the article, "Jesus' Yoke and Burden," by David Bivin, which is available at www.JerusalemPerspective.com.

5.

How Jesus' Words Were Preserved

How did the teachings of Jesus become our Gospels? How reliable are they at preserving Jesus' words? Why are many of Jesus' sayings in a different order in each Gospel? We can have a much better understanding of how the Gospels were written by looking at the unusual method used by first-century rabbis to accurately preserve their sayings over time.

It may surprise us that a disciple of a sage was not permitted to transmit in writing the words of his master.[1] A rabbi's teaching was considered "Oral Torah" (inspired, authoritative Scripture interpretation), and as such its transmission in writing was strongly prohibited. It therefore seems likely that Jesus' first disciples would not have dared preserve his teaching in writing, but would have transmitted it orally. Rather than compromising Jesus' words, this was more likely key to preserving them accurately for future generations.

The Accuracy of Oral Transmission

We tend to view orally transmitted material as less trustworthy than material transmitted in writing. This is because we are familiar only with the oral transmission of myths such as Viking sagas, which were modified with each retelling. The so-called "Oral Hypothesis," accepted by most New Testament scholars for nearly a century, is based on the assumption that gospel stories, faint memories of the original Semitic stories, are an oral development within the early Greek-speaking church. It is taken for granted that these stories were embellished by Greek-speaking teachers and preachers, growing to their present size as they were told and retold, only to be written down in Greek decades after the death of Jesus.

Oral transmission in rabbinic circles within first-century Jewish society was not at all like this. The transmission of oral literature by rabbis and their disciples approached 100% accuracy, far greater accuracy than could be achieved through written transmission. When literature is transmitted in hand-copied documents, inevitably mistakes known as "scribal errors" creep in. The rabbis were aware of this danger. They knew that if their literature were transmitted in writing, it would lose its high degree of accuracy. Therefore, they forbade its written transmission.[2]

To illustrate, consider this version of Matthew 6:10: "Thy kingdom come, my will be done on earth as it is in heaven...." Because most Christians recall this line from memory, the smallest error leaps out. Similarly, when a saying is repeated orally in a community where it is known by several members, together they insure its accuracy. But if a saying is only preserved and transmitted in handwriting, the self-correction is absent. Any errors would unknowingly be perpetuated.

It is hard for us to appreciate the trustworthiness and accuracy of oral transmission within rabbinic circles of the first century. The disciple of a sage was not permitted to alter even one word of a tradition he had received from his teacher when quoting him to others.[3] The disciple was also required to cite his sources. Thus, many rabbinic sayings are introduced, "Rabbi Y in the name of Rabbi X," in other words, "Rabbi Y, who is transmitting a tradition he has received from Rabbi X." It also is hard for us to appreciate the volume of orally transmitted material that disciples of a first-century rabbi had committed to memory. They knew an enormous amount of oral literature, including the Scriptures, the way Christians know the Lord's Prayer.

Pursuing this line of reasoning, one can suggest that the first written collection of Jesus' words and deeds was a Greek work, which may have been a translation of an oral Hebrew collection of Jesus' deeds and teaching, memorized by Jesus' first disciples and transmitted by them with a high degree of accuracy. Perhaps an early bilingual follower of the Way compiled this collection as he sat listening day by day to the Hebrew sermons and lessons of the Twelve or one of the other disciples who had been with Jesus from the beginning of his public ministry (Acts 1:21–22). As the Twelve preached and taught, they interspersed in their presentations many of the deeds and sayings of Jesus. Perhaps the listener took notes in Hebrew and later translated them to Greek, or simply translated what he heard directly into Greek.

This anonymous, bilingual listener may have been John Mark. Papias, bishop of Hierapolis in Asia Minor during the mid-second century A.D., wrote:

> Mark, who was Peter's interpreter, wrote down accurately what he remembered. He did not, however, report the sayings or deeds of the Lord in their exact order. For he had not heard the Lord nor accompanied him, but Peter, later, as he said. Peter adapted his teaching to the needs [of his listeners] making no attempt to give a connected whole of the Lord's sayings. Thus, Mark did not act wrongly in writing certain things as he remembered them. For he had one concern only: to omit nothing of what he had heard and write nothing untrue.[4]

It is difficult to know how much confidence to place in the traditions of Papias. However, according to Papias, Mark served as Peter's translator, and wrote down Peter's teaching as he remembered it. Mark's account was not chronologically ordered because Peter's teaching was not a continuous narrative.[5]

A modern scribe with quill making repairs to a Torah scroll, Jaffa, 1960.

Differences in the Order of Jesus' Sayings

The Twelve, along with the other disciples who had studied with Jesus, knew his entire biography by heart; however, when they taught or preached they did not present it in chronological fashion. Rather, they incorporated accounts of Jesus' deeds and sections of his teaching within their own expositions. For example, an apostle may have incorporated in his sermon only one of two twin parables with which Jesus originally concluded a teaching, since only one of the parables fit the sermon's theme. Though the stories of Jesus' Hebrew biography were preached and taught piecemeal, as long as they were transmitted orally, they were accurately preserved.

The authors of Matthew, Mark and Luke all tried to arrange the stories in their Gospels chronologically. Though they contain many of the same stories, the gospel writers do not always present their common stories in the same order. For example, there are forty-seven stories found exclusively in Matthew and Luke, yet the two authors agree only once on where to place these stories. A major reason for the writing of these accounts was perhaps the authors' feeling that their own source material lacked chronological order. The author of Luke states that the reason for his writing was to provide a certain Theophilus with an orderly account. It is significant that it is Greek writers, with their culture's ideal of order, who feel the need for an "orderly account" of Jesus' life.

Most likely, the earliest documents containing Jesus' teachings had a great concern for accurate quotation, but little interest in preserving sayings or stories within their original context. Arranging sacred history without an interest in its order of progression, though against the sensibilities of modern, non-Jewish readers of the Bible, was common in ancient Judaism. Tying a story or saying to a verse of Scripture took precedence over preserving the authentic historical context. For instance, in the books of Isaiah, Jeremiah and Ezekiel, events in the lives of those prophets are not recorded in order.[6] Concern for chronological order was simply not an overriding consideration.

The protocol of the world of an ancient sage and his disciples may explain why many of the acts and sayings of Jesus in the Gospels have been divorced from their original settings. The first written "Life of Jesus" may have been a Greek document composed by a bilingual disciple whose account was based upon the oral teaching delivered in Hebrew by one or more of the twelve apostles and other former full-time apprentices of Jesus. Explaining the origin of the differences in the story orders of Matthew, Mark and Luke is one of the New Testament scholar's greatest challenges.

---

[1] A unique feature of a Pharisaic rabbi's method of study was the use of memorized sources. When students and teachers from other streams of first-century Judaism engaged in study, they made use of scrolls. The Essenes, for example, preserved their teaching in writing, and made use of scrolls when studying. The Pharisees, however, brought no scrolls to class. Instead, they brought well-memorized Scriptures and oral traditions. The material put forward for discussion by Pharisaic rabbis and students came from their mental storehouses. Apparently, Jesus belonged to a stream within Judaism that was closely related to the Pharisees. See "Jesus and the Pharisees" (pp. 3–4) in Shmuel Safrai's "Jesus and the Hasidim," *Jerusalem Perspective* 42, 43 & 44 (Jan–Jun 1994), pp. 3–22.

In the first century A.D. the literature of the Pharisees was transmitted orally. Later, around A.D. 200, the term "Oral Torah" was used to describe this literature, which was considered authoritative commentary on the written Torah. (See Shmuel Safrai, "Literary Languages in the Time of Jesus," *Jerusalem Perspective* 31 [Mar/Apr 1991], p. 3).

[2] The prohibition against committing to writing words transmitted orally is found in the Babylonian Talmud (b. Gittin 60b). This prohibition also applied to the writing of blessings and prayers (t. Shabbat 13:4).

[3] "A person must always transmit a tradition in the same words in which he received it from his teacher" (m. Eduyot 1:3).

[4] Eusebius, *Ecclesiastical History III*, 39, 15. Papias also wrote that "Matthew put down the words [of the Lord] in the Hebrew language, and others have translated them, each as best he could" (*Ecclesiastical History III*, 39, 16). The Papias tradition about Matthew, together with the Synoptic Gospels' Semitic flavor, caused Robert Lindsey of the Jerusalem School, to posit a written Hebrew source. *(The Jesus Sources: Understanding the Gospels* [Tulsa, OK: HaKesher, 1990], p. 13; *Jesus Rabbi & Lord: The Hebrew Story of Jesus Behind Our Gospels* [Oak Creek, WI: Cornerstone Publishing, 1990], p. 207).

[5] The document to which Papias refers is not necessarily identical with the canonical Gospel of Mark.

[6] The rabbis maintained that events in the Torah are not necessarily

arranged according to chronological order: "There is no chronological order [literally, 'early and late'] in the Torah" (j. Megillah 70b, b. Pesahim 6b).

"How Jesus' Words Were Preserved" was adapted and abridged from the article, "The Discomposure of Jesus' Biography," by David Bivin, available at www.JerusalemPerspective.com.

II.
Jesus' First-Century Jewish Context

6.

Jesus Within Jewish Practice

How observant was Jesus of the rulings of other rabbis of his day, later called the "Oral Torah?" Some have assumed that he rejected their teachings, but a closer reading shows that he lived within the laws and traditions of his time. Knowing more about these traditions and how Jesus interacted with them can help us understand him much better.

The Oral Torah

Torah has always been the focus of rabbinic teaching. Unfortunately, the Hebrew word *torah* is usually translated in English simply as "law," which has created the impression that it has to do only with commandments. This is not the case at all. The Torah was given by God as a set of guidelines for a whole way of life. A better translation would be "God's instructions."

Written Torah consists of the instruction God gave to Israel at Sinai contained in the five books of Moses — Genesis, Exodus, Leviticus, Numbers and Deuteronomy. The rabbis were the creators of the Oral Torah — commentary and legal interpretation of its instructions for daily living. This literature, still unwritten in Jesus' day, is of great value in understanding Jesus' sayings.

The Oral Torah was a living tradition with the authority to interpret and at times modify the written code. A contemporary analogy is found in the body of legal precedent that develops as judges hand down rulings which interpret the laws enacted by legislators. Such judges, like the early rabbis, apply the written law as cases are brought before them, and thus create a tradition of interpretations and precedents that is no less authoritative than are the laws themselves.

As the name implies, the Oral Torah was transmitted orally and, in the time of Jesus, was still unwritten. It was only after Jewish life in

Israel had been nearly extinguished that this literature was recorded in writing in the Mishnah, compiled by Rabbi Yehudah ha-Nasi around A.D. 200. The Mishnah records the sayings of sages who lived and taught during the previous several hundred years and, except for isolated words or sentences, it is written entirely in Hebrew.

Once Rabbi Yehudah broke with tradition, other collections of the Oral Torah were made, notably the Gemara, which is a commentary on the Mishnah. In time, the Gemara and Mishnah were printed together as the Talmud. Although these works contain rabbinic traditions unwritten before the third century A.D., these traditions can be reliable testimony for the historical reality of the Second Temple period, when Jesus lived.[1]

The Talmud exists in two versions: the Jerusalem Talmud, compiled in Israel in about A.D. 400.; and the Babylonian Talmud, compiled by Jewish rabbis in Babylonia about one hundred years later. This second work is a gigantic sea of rabbinic learning, consisting of two and one-half million words, filling 5,894 pages. Today the Babylonian Talmud is still central in Jewish religious education.

Parallels in the Sayings of the Fathers

The best-known of the Mishnah's sixty-three tractates is titled "Pirke Avot" (Chapters of the Fathers) or simply "Avot" (meaning "fathers") but it is often referred to in English as the "Sayings of the Fathers" or "Ethics of the Fathers." Avot is a collection of the cherished sayings of more than sixty illustrious rabbis, beginning with sayings from the third century B.C. Although the subject matter of the rest of the Mishnah is primarily legal, Avot is devotional in nature, dealing almost wholly with moral behavior. Only six chapters in length, this tractate has some of the closest parallels to the sayings of Jesus known from rabbinic literature.[2]

For example, one saying is, "The day is short and the work is great, but the workers are lazy; however the wages are high since the owner is in a hurry."[3] This is close to Jesus' words in Matthew 9:37–38: "The [work of] harvesting is great and the workers are few.

Ask the owner of the harvest to bring [more] workers for his harvest."

Another passage reads, "Do not be like slaves that serve their master in order to receive a reward; rather, be like slaves that do not serve their master in order to receive a reward" (m. Avot 1:3). This seems to parallel Jesus' saying, "...So you too, when you have done all the things you are commanded, say, 'We are unworthy slaves. We have only done what it was our duty to do'" (Lk 17:7-8, 10).

Equally as important as Avot's parallels are its sayings that describe the religious lifestyle of Jesus' time, particularly the life of the rabbi and disciple. The very first passage of the tractate exhorts rabbis to "Raise up many disciples" (m. Avot 1:1), a parallel to Jesus' words to "make disciples of all nations" (Mt 28:19). Another line calls upon the people to show hospitality to rabbis: "Let your home be a meeting place for the rabbis, and cover yourself with the dust of their feet, and drink in their words thirstily."[4]

This is the first page of the Babylonian Talmud in the Vilna edition. The core text of the Mishnah and Talmud are in the center surrounded by notes and commentaries. The entire work is almost 6,000 pages in length.

We can see that Mary and Martha followed these instructions and opened their home to Jesus and his disciples (Lk 10:38-42). Yet other sayings describe the typical life of a Jewish man in Jesus' day, showing the emphasis on education and study of the Scriptures.[5]

A number of sayings in Avot, although not directly parallel to sayings of Jesus, strongly remind us of the spiritual depth found in Jesus' teaching:

This world is like an entry hall before the world to come. Prepare yourself in the entry hall that you may enter into the banqueting hall. (m. Avot 4:16)

Be as strong as the leopard, swift as the eagle, fleet as the gazelle and brave as the lion to do the will of your Father in heaven. (m. Avot 5:20)[6]

Jesus and the Practice of Blessing

To what extent did Jesus observe the practices of the Oral Torah? Jesus was never charged with breaking any of them, and although his disciples occasionally were accused of disobeying aspects of the Oral Torah (Lk 6:1–2), only one such accusation was made against Jesus — that he broke the Sabbath by healing the sick (Lk 14:1–4). However, even his Sabbath healings were permitted by rabbinic ruling.[7]

It may seem that there is a shortage of hard evidence in the New Testament concerning Jesus' religious observance, but one must remember that the New Testament was written by Jews for Jewish readers. The normal Jewish religious practices were so well known and followed both by the writers and first readers of the New Testament, that it would have been considered superfluous to discuss them. Nonetheless, one is able to gather enough evidence from the Gospels to conclude that Jesus observed the biblical commandments as they were interpreted in the Oral Torah.

Jesus apparently attached great importance to the Oral Torah (unwritten in his day), and it seems he considered it to be authoritative. When he admonished his disciples to "do and observe everything they [the scribes and Pharisees] command you" (Mt 23:3), he was referring to the Pharisees' oral traditions and interpretations of the Written Torah. The Written Torah itself could not have been in question, for it was accepted by all sects of Judaism, and Jesus himself said, "Heaven and earth would sooner disappear than one yod (the smallest letter in the Hebrew alphabet) or even one kots (thorn, the long, thorn-like decorative stroke that first-century scribes added to the yod) from the Torah" (Mt 5:18). Many rabbinic statements express similar ideas, such as: "Should all the nations of the world unite to uproot one word of the Torah, they would be unable to do it."[8]

Blessings for all Occasions

One of the most basic examples of a rabbinic command that Jesus obeyed is in the realm of blessings. The sole scriptural basis for the many blessings that an observant Jew still says daily is Deuteronomy 8:10:

> When you have eaten your fill, thank the LORD your God...(literally, "And you will eat and you will be full and you will bless the LORD your God").

The rabbis found justification in this verse for saying a blessing before the meal as well as after, and on many other occasions — indeed, on almost every occasion. The general rabbinic rule was, "Anything that is enjoyed requires a blessing."[9]

> If a man built a house or bought something new he was to say, "Blessed is he who has brought us to this moment." If one saw a place where great miracles had occurred in Israel's history, one was to say, "Blessed is he who in this place performed miracles for our ancestors." In response to a shooting star, lightning, a storm or an earthquake, one was to say, "Blessed is he whose strength fills the universe"; and a mountain, hill, lake, river or desert were to prompt, "Blessed is he who fashions the works of creation."[10]

There was a blessing to be said before publicly reading from the Torah, and another at the completion of the reading; a blessing after immersing oneself in a *mikveh* (ritual immersion bath); and a blessing upon seeing a great scholar. One was obligated to bless God for calamity and misfortune as well as for prosperity and good fortune: For rain and for good news one says, "Blessed is he who is good and who gives good." For bad news one says, "Blessed is he who is the faithful judge."

There is evidence that Jesus adhered to the rulings of the Oral Torah in his use of various blessings. Blessing God for food after eating is a biblical commandment. But, Jesus also said a blessing before eating. Blessing before the meal is a commandment of the Oral Torah, or more precisely, a rabbinic interpretation of a commandment in the Written Torah.

In conformity with the rabbinic interpretation of Deuteronomy 8:10, Jesus not only recited a blessing after meals, but also said the blessing before meals: *baruch hamotsi lechem min haarets* (Blessed is he who brings bread out of the earth). It is recorded that at the last Passover meal that Jesus ate with his disciples in Jerusalem, Jesus "took bread and blessed and broke and gave to his disciples" (Mt 26:26).

Since in the Greek text there is no direct object following the verbs "blessed," "broke" and "gave," English translators have felt it necessary to supply the word "it" after each of these, or at least after "broke" and "gave." The English reader therefore receives the impression that Jesus not only divided and distributed the bread, but blessed it as well. This is simply a misunderstanding. In the context of taking a loaf of bread before beginning a meal, the blessing can only be a blessing directed toward God.

Before dining with the two disciples from Emmaus, Jesus "blessed, broke and gave," as he did before he fed the five thousand with five loaves and two fish (In Luke's account, but not in Mark's or Matthew's, the text reads "blessed them," but one important Greek manuscript reads "blessed for them" at Luke 9:16.) Because of the recurring "blessed, broke and gave the bread" in the Gospels, it is a common Christian misunderstanding that Jesus blessed the bread. Consequently, Christians customarily "bless the food" before they eat a meal.

The blessing that was said in Jesus' time before one ate was praise and thanksgiving to God who so wondrously provides food for his children, to him who "brings bread out of the earth." One does not bless the food, nor does one even ask God to bless the food. One blesses God who provides the food. This is a good example of how Christians' lack of knowledge of Jewish custom has led to misunderstanding an act of Jesus. In this case it has led to the development of a Christian practice that, though perhaps not harmful in itself, has no foundation whatsoever in Jesus' own practice or teaching.

It is similarly a misunderstanding to assume that Jesus multiplied the loaves and fish by blessing them. Jesus, as usual, simply blessed God before beginning the meal. The miracle was not in the blessing, for food did not multiply on other occasions when Jesus offered a blessing before breaking bread.

Luke made it clearer for his Greek-speaking readers when he described Paul's practice of "saying grace." A literal translation of Acts 27:35 reads: "And taking bread, he gave thanks to God before all, and breaking, he began to eat."

---

[1] Shmuel Safrai, "Talmudic Literature as an Historical Source for the Second Temple Period," *Mishkan* 17–18 (1993), pp. 121–137.

[2] Apart from the Bible, the Prayer Book and the Passover Haggadah, *Avot* is probably better known to religious Jews that any other book, and more commentaries have been written on *Avot* than on any other rabbinic work. Even less religiously-learned Jews are familiar with the maxims contained in *Avot*. It is so popular that it has become a custom to study a chapter of it in the synagogue following the afternoon prayers each Saturday between Passover and the Jewish New Year (a five-month period). Consequently, the entire tractate is included in editions of the Prayer Book.

[3] M. Avot 2:15, from Rabbi Tarfon (born c. A.D. 50–55).

[4] M. Avot 1:4, from Yose ben Yoezer, who lived in the first half of the second century B.C., about 200 years before Jesus. See pp. 12–14 and footnotes for more discussion.

[5] M. Avot 5:21. See pp. 4–5 for more discussion.

[6] For other treasures of rabbinic literature, see the following anthologies of rabbinic quotations: Abraham Cohen, *Everyman's Talmud*, 2nd ed. (1949; reprinted New York: Schocken Books, 1975); Claude Montefiore and Herbert Loewe, *A Rabbinic Anthology* (1938; reprinted New York: Schocken Books 1974).

[7] Shmuel Safrai, "Religion in Everyday Life," in *The Jewish People in the First Century* (ed. Shmuel Safrai and Menahem Stern; Amsterdam: Van Gorcum, 1976), p. 805.

[8] Leviticus Rabbah 19:2. For more discussion about Mt 5:18 and Jesus' words about the law, see pp. 94–96.

[9] B. Berachot 35a.

[10] There was even a blessing to be said when one urinated: "Blessed is he who formed man in wisdom and created in him numerous orifices and cavities. It is revealed and known before the throne of your glory that if even one of them should be opened or if even one of them should be obstructed, it would be impossible to exist and stand before you" (b. Berachot 60b).

"Jesus Within Jewish Practice" was adapted and abridged from the following articles by David Bivin, at www.JerusalemPerspective.com: "Written and Oral Torah," "Jesus and the Oral Torah: Blessing," and "Rabbinic Literature: A Spiritual Treasure."

7.

Of Hems, Tassels and Tefillin

And behold, a woman which was diseased with an issue of blood twelve years came behind him and touched the hem of his garment. For she said within herself, If I but touch his garment, I shall be whole. (Mt 9:20–21, KJV)

The New Testament makes it clear that Jesus, like all observant Jews of the first century, wore *tzitziyot*. These are the tassels that were attached to the four corners of one's robe as commanded in Numbers 15:37–41 and Deuteronomy 22:12.

Jesus' observance of this commandment is dramatically illustrated by the story, found in Matthew 9, Mark 5 and Luke 8, of the woman who suffered from a hemorrhage for twelve years. She was healed when she came up behind Jesus and touched what the King James Version of the Bible refers to as "hem of his garment."

If this story originally existed in Hebrew, then it seems certain that it was not the hem, but one of the *tzitziyot* of Jesus' garment that the woman touched. The Greek word that the King James translators rendered "hem" is *kraspedon*. This is the same word that is used in the Septuagint, the ancient Greek translation of the Hebrew Scriptures, to translate *tzitzit* (the singular of *tzitziyot*). It is found three times in Numbers 15:37–41, where the wearing of *tzitziyot* is commanded. In Hebrew, therefore, the story would have spoken of the woman touching the *tzitziyot talito*, that is the *tzitzit* (tassel) of his *talit* (mantle).

Apparently, most human beings need to be reminded of God and the observance of his commandments, and the wearing of *tzitziyot* might be compared to tying a string around one's finger. According to Numbers 15:39, these tassels served as a sign to help the wearers "recall all the commandments of the LORD and observe them so that you do not follow the lustful desires of your heart and eyes."

There was no fixed maximum length for the *tzitziyot*,[1] but it seems there were some who, in an attempt to observe this commandment more fully, wore very long *tzitziyot*. A wealthy Jerusalem resident is mentioned in the Talmud who received his nickname, Ben Tzitzit Hakeset, because of his long tassels. He was remembered as being so devout that his *tzitziyot* literally trailed behind him on the ground.[2] Naturally, there also were imitators, who wished to appear more pious than they were by wearing longer-than-normal *tzitziyot*. Jesus condemned those who pretended to be pious by wearing long *tzitziyot* (Mt 23:5).

First-Century Garments

Like his Mediterranean contemporaries, Jesus wore two garments, a *haluk* — a tunic, and a *talit* — a mantle. The lower garment, the tunic, was a lighter robe, usually made of linen. The upper garment, the mantle, which was draped over the tunic, was a heavy garment, usually woven from wool. The *talit* was a rectangular piece of cloth. It was the equivalent of the Roman *pallium* or the Greek *himation*, which were rectangular, not the Roman toga, which was semi-circular.

The heavier outer garment was the norm for public occasions. It was considered somewhat immodest in Jewish society to go out in public attired only in the under-robe, even though it extended to just above the ankles. The *haluk* alone could be worn around the house (unless guests arrived), or when one engaged in physical labor where the over-robe would be too cumbersome.

Under the influence of what is called *talit* by Jews of today, some translators have understood that the *talit* was a shawl-like covering draped over the upper part of a man's body during prayer. For instance, in Matthew 23:5, the New International Version translates, "They make...the tassels of their prayer shawls long." This is misleading since, in the time of Jesus, the *talit* was part of everyday dress and not a religious article. It is true that out of modesty one would not pray publicly in his *haluk*, but the *talit* was not itself a holy garment.

This clarification of the double robes worn in Jesus' time helps us understand his statement recorded in Matthew 5:40, "If someone wants to sue you for your *haluk*, let him also have your *talit.*" In the privacy of one's home, the *haluk* could be worn without the *talit,* but it was embarrassing to go out in public dressed in it alone. However, if necessary, the *talit* could serve as one's only garment. Therefore, the *talit* rather than the *haluk* was indispensable.

If someone tries to confiscate your tunic in a dispute, Jesus said, you should, for the sake of peace, also offer him your mantle.

Tefillin — Phylacteries

The Gospels attest to the fact that Jesus had tassels on the four corners of his outer robe (Mt 9:20; Mt 14:36; Mk 6:56; Lk 8:44). Although there is no explicit evidence in the Gospels, we have reason to suggest that he also may have worn phylacteries. The word "phylactery" is derived from the Greek *phylakterion,* and literally means a protecting charm or amulet. "Phylacteries" is an unfortunate translation, as there is little if any evidence to suggest that they were regarded as amulets in Jesus' day. The Hebrew word is *tefillin* (the plural of *tefillah,* prayer).

Tefillin refers to either of the two small leather capsules containing tiny slips of parchment inscribed with the scriptural passages recorded in Exodus 13:1-10, Exodus 13:11-16, Deuteronomy 6:4-9, and Deuteronomy 11:13-21. Today, as in Jesus' day, the *tefillin* are strapped on the forehead and the arm. The arm *tefillin* consists of one compartment containing a parchment on which all four passages are written, while the head *tefillin* is divided into four compartments, each of which contains a parchment with one of the four

A modern wearer of tefillin

passages written on it.

Wearing *tefillin* was an observance of the commandment to bind God's commandments "as a sign on your arm and as a symbol on your forehead" (Deut 6:4-9; Deut 11:18-21). It might be argued that this is metaphorical language and simply means "remember well." For example, the same expression is used in Exodus 13:16. There, following the commandment to sacrifice every firstborn male animal and redeem every firstborn male child, the Israelites are informed that "it will be a sign on your arm and a symbol on your forehead." Obviously, this observance could not be attached to one's body. However, by at least the second century B.C., the biblical instructions to bind the commandments of the LORD to one's arm and forehead were interpreted literally.[3]

Contemporaries of Jesus would have viewed the wearing of tefillin as a biblical commandment, but in fact, the literal understanding of this commandment is an interpretation, part of the Oral Torah. The word *tefillin* itself is not even found in the Bible.

Worn Every Day

In the first century, *tefillin* were part of ordinary everyday Jewish dress. Putting on *tefillin* only during morning weekday prayers, as normally practiced today by observant Jews, is a later custom. In Jesus' time, they were worn throughout the day, and removed only when working or when entering a place that was ritually unclean.[4]

Fragments of *tefillin* dating from the time of Jesus have been found in the Judean Desert in caves near the Dead Sea. The most dramatic find, head *tefillin* dating from the first half of the first century A.D. were found at Qumran, with three of the four parchment slips still folded and securely tied in their original compartments.[5]

The head *tefillin,* including the strap, was quite modest and would not have drawn attention to itself. The capsule found at Qumran is rectangular and extremely small, approximately one-half by three-fourths of an inch (13 by 20 mm). A small postage stamp would easily cover it.

In Matthew 23:5, Jesus criticized those who "make their phylacteries wide." As with his criticism of the public display of almsgiving (Mt 6:2), one must not view Jesus' words as a general condemnation of wearing *tefillin*. Rather, Jesus was condemning religious hypocrisy that led to enlarging *tefillin* as a demonstration of "higher spirituality."

Just as Jesus faulted the ostentatious wearing of *tzitziyot* (tassels), which he himself wore, he probably also was wearing *tefillin* while criticizing those who wore them hypocritically. Had he not worn *tefillin*, it is unlikely that his criticism would have been directed only at the excesses. Criticizing the way they were worn implies Jesus' acceptance of the practice and the sages' literal interpretation of this biblical command.

---

[1] "The elders of the School of Shammai and the School of Hillel gathered in the upper chambers of Jonathan ben Bathyra and reached the decision that there is no prescribed length for the *tzitzit*." (Sifre Numbers 115, to 15:38).

[2] B. Gittin 56a; Shmuel Safrai, *The Jewish People in the First Century*, p. 798, note 3.

[3] Shmuel Safrai, *The Jewish People in the First Century*, p. 799.

[4] Safrai, p. 798.

[5] Yigael Yadin, *Tefillin from Qumran* (Israel Exploration Society, 1969).

"Of Hems, Tassels and Tefillin" was adapted and abridged from "Jesus and the Oral Torah: The Hem of His Garment," and "Jesus and the Oral Torah: Did Jesus Wear Phylacteries?" by David Bivin, available at www.JerusalemPerspective.com.

8.

Jesus and the Unutterable Name of God

Another example of Jesus' observance of the Oral Torah, the traditions and rulings of Jewish rabbis before him, is his adherence to the rabbinic prohibition against using the unutterable name of God. For thousands of years, Jews have regarded the name of God as too holy to be spoken out loud. We may be surprised that Jesus treated God's name with the same reverence as the rest of his people did over the ages.

The original understanding of the third commandment, "You shall not take the name of the Lord your God in vain" (Ex 20:7), was that one must keep one's vow when swearing by God's name. The rabbis eventually came to interpret this commandment to mean using the Lord's name lightly or frivolously. To avoid the risk of employing the divine name irreverently, the rabbis ruled that one should not utter it at all.

In Jesus' time, the tetragrammaton, YHWH,[1] could be pronounced only in the Temple, in the daily priestly blessing and in the confession of the High Priest on the Day of Atonement.[2] So serious was the prohibition against pronouncing the tetragrammaton, that the rabbis included among those who have no share in the World to Come "he who pronounces the Divine Name as it is spelled."[3] When reading or reciting Scripture, one was not to pronounce the Unutterable Name, but rather to substitute *Adonai*, Lord, literally, "my lords."

This avoidance of the tetragrammaton began very early. Although there was no hesitation about pronouncing the Sacred Name in daily life during the First Temple period at least until the Babylonian Exile in 586 B.C., already by the third century B.C. *Adonai* was being substituted for YHWH.[4]

In time, the substitute *Adonai* itself came to have such a sacred aura that it was used only in Scripture reading and prayer. When it was necessary to refer to God in everyday speech, other substitutes were sought: *hashem* (the Name), *hamakom* (the Place), *hagavoah* (the High), *halashon* (the Tongue), *shamayim* (Heaven), and others. Even *Elohim*, (God), which could refer to the God of Israel or to false gods, was avoided in conversation. This tradition continues until today, even among many secular Jews. The more orthodox even say *"Elokim"* in order to avoid saying *Elohim*, and Jews often write "G-d" instead of "God."

Jehovah: A Christian Misunderstanding

In any attempt to understand the Bible, there is no substitute for a knowledge of ancient Jewish custom and practice. For example, the term "Jehovah," which is found in many Christian translations of the Bible, originated because of a lack of awareness of Jewish custom.

Until the early Middle Ages, Hebrew was written without vowels. But by the sixth century A.D. there were only a few native Hebrew speakers left, and most Jews had only a passive knowledge of Hebrew. It was then that a system of vowel signs was developed by the Masoretes, the Jewish scholars of the period, to aid the reader in pronunciation. In accordance with the custom observed since the third century B.C., when reading or reciting Scripture, they superimposed the vowel signs of the word *Adonai* upon the four consonants of God's name. This was to remind the reader he should not attempt to pronounce the unutterable name. Thus *YHWH* would be read as *Adonai*.[5]

When Christian scholars in Europe first began to study Hebrew, they misunderstood this warning device. Lacking even the most elementary knowledge of Jewish culture and custom, they fused the vowels of *Adonai* with the consonants of the divine name and thus gave the Church "Jehovah," a word which has no meaning in Hebrew.[6] The first consonant of the word, the "y" sound, was transliterated by "j" in Latin, and the third consonant, the "w" sound, by "v."

I believe that as Christians we should be sensitive to this ancient Jewish tradition. To our embarrassment, we continue to perpetuate this error in Christian books, hymns, songs and translations of the Bible.[7] The non-word "Jehovah" would be simply an amusing mistake if it did not illustrate so vividly Christians' continuing lack of understanding of Hebrew language and Jewish practice.

Jesus' Reverence for the Name

Jesus often used euphemisms for God — his audiences would have been shocked had he not. The most common word for God used by Jesus was "Heaven." This occurs often throughout the Gospel of Matthew in the phrase "Kingdom of Heaven," the term Jesus used for his community of disciples.

Mark and Luke used "Kingdom of God," possibly because most of their Greek readers might not have understood the euphemism. The original, however, is *malchut shamayim* (Kingdom of Heaven), which is common in the Hebrew literature of the period while "Kingdom of God" is never used.

Matthew 21:25 quotes Jesus asking those in the Temple who questioned his authority, "Was the baptism of John from Heaven [i.e., from God] or from men?" Similarly, in the parable of the prodigal son (Lk 15:21), Jesus had the prodigal say to his father, "I have sinned against Heaven."

One other euphemism for God's name used by Jesus was *hagvurah*, (the Power). When interrogated by the high priests, Jesus was asked to admit that he was the Messiah. His answer, recorded in Matthew 26:64 and Luke 22:69, is a classic example of rabbinic sophistication: "From now on the 'Son of Man' will be sitting on the right of the Power," which hints at two messianic passages from Scripture, Daniel 7:13 and Psalm 110:1. Even though Jesus was deferentially referring to God in an oblique way, everyone would have realized that he was making a powerful claim to be the promised Messiah, the Son of God.

---

[1] By linguistic comparisons with other ancient Semitic languages, scholars can be almost certain that the divine name was originally pronounced "yah·WEH." The pronunciation of the first syllable of the tetragrammaton is confirmed by the abbreviated form of God's name *yah* (transcribed "Jah" in the King James Version), which is sometimes used in biblical poetry (Ps 68:4). It is also confirmed by the *yah* which is

attached as a suffix to many Hebrew names such as *eliyah,* Elijah and *ovadyah,* Obadiah.

[2] Sifre Numbers 39; m. Sotah 7:6; m. Yoma 6:2.

[3] M. Sanhedrin 10:1; cf. 7:5.

[4] Louis F. Hartman, "Names of God," in *Encyclopaedia Judaica* (Jerusalem: Keter Publishing House, 1971), 7:680. See also Ray Pritz, "The Divine Name in the Hebrew New Testament," *Jerusalem Perspective* 31 (Mar/Apr 1991), pp. 10–12.

[5] There is one small difference between the vowels of *Adonai* and those of the tetragrammaton. The Masoretes altered the "*ah*" vowel of the first syllable so that readers would not see "*yah*" and inadvertently blurt out the unutterable name.

If the tetragrammaton happened to appear in the biblical text either before or after the word *Adonai,* then the Masoretes superimposed the vowels of *Elohim* upon the tetragrammaton *YHWH* (to be read *Elohim*). Thus these two combinations, *Adonai YHWH* and *YHWH Adonai,* were pronounced *Elohim Adonai* and *Adonai Elohim* respectively. In English translations of the Bible they are usually translated "the LORD God" and "Lord GOD."

[6] The mistake was first made by Italian theologian and Franciscan friar Galatinus in A.D. 1518, in his *De arcanis catholicae veritatis,* a monumental work of Christian mysticism. See Godfrey Edmond Silverman, "Galatinus, Pietro (Petrus) Columna," in *Encyclopaedia Judaica,* 7:262–263.

[7] The American Standard Version and The Living Bible use "Jehovah" for YHWH throughout, while translations such as the King James Version, New English Bible, and New Berkeley Version use "Jehovah" only occasionally.

"Jesus and the Unutterable Name of God" was adapted and abridged from "Oral Torah: The Unutterable Name of God," and "'Jehovah'—A Christian Misunderstanding," by David Bivin, which are available online at www.JerusalemPerspective.com.

9.

The Jewish Prayers of Jesus

The prayer that Jesus taught his disciples (Mt 6:9–13; Lk 11:2–4) is viewed by Christians as a model prayer. It is even sometimes suggested that since the Lord's Prayer can easily be prayed in about half a minute, prayers should be kept to that length. A little Jewish background on the prayers of Jesus' day provides an important perspective on the Lord's Prayer.

The Central Prayer of Jewish Life

The central prayer in Jewish life and liturgy is known by a number of names: *Shemoneh Esreh* (Eighteen), since it originally consisted of eighteen benedictions; *Amidah* (Standing), because it is said standing; or simply *Tefillah* (Prayer), the prayer par excellence. It is very ancient, its final version dating from around A.D. 90–100 when a nineteenth benediction was added.

This prayer is the essential part of the morning, afternoon and evening weekday services in the synagogue. It is said first in a whisper by the worshipers and then recited aloud by the reader. The prayer is composed of three opening benedictions of praise which include "We will hallow your name in the world as it is hallowed in the highest heavens"; thirteen petitions including petitions for wisdom, healing, forgiveness, deliverance from want and affliction, and for the sending of the Messiah, "the branch of David"; and three concluding benedictions which include thanksgiving to the "rock of our lives and shield of our salvation" whose "miracles are daily with us," whose "wonders and benefits occur evening, morning and noon," and whose "mercies and kindnesses never cease." A person who is fluent in Hebrew can pray this prayer in about five minutes.

Every Jew is religiously obligated to pray the Eighteen Benedictions daily.[1] In times of emergency, however, this obligation is fulfilled by praying a shortened, summary form of the Eighteen, for example:

> O Lord, save your people the remnant of Israel; in every time of crisis may their needs not be lost sight of by you. Blessed are you, O Lord, who answers prayer.[2]

Other rabbis taught their disciples short summary prayers.[3] Rabbi Eliezer (a younger contemporary of Jesus) said:

> May your will be done in heaven above, grant peace of mind to those who fear you [on earth] below, and do what seems best to you. Blessed are you, O Lord, who answers prayer.

Note the phrases "your will be done" and "in heaven above ... [on earth] below" as in the Lord's Prayer. Also note the parallel between "grant peace of mind" in the prayer Eliezer taught and "deliver us from evil" in the Lord's Prayer. The Babylonian Talmud, Berachot 29b provides additional examples of abbreviated prayers:

> Rabbi Yehoshua says: "Hear the supplication of your people Israel and quickly fulfill their request. Blessed are you, O Lord, who answers prayer."

> Rabbi Eleazar son of Rabbi Zadok says: "Hear the cry of your people Israel and quickly fulfill their request. Blessed are you, O Lord, who answers prayer."

> Other sages say: "The needs of your people Israel are many but they do not know how to ask for their needs. May it be your will, O Lord our God, to sustain each and every one and to supply each person what is needed. Blessed are you, O Lord, who answers prayer."

The petitions for God's provision for livelihood and his supply of what is needed are strongly reminiscent of the request for "daily bread" in the Lord's Prayer.

The rabbis taught their disciples abbreviated versions of the Eighteen Benedictions such as those above, and it seems likely that Jesus did too. Far from being proof that customarily one should pray very brief prayers, the Lord's Prayer points us to the Eighteen. It can be assumed that Jesus and his disciples prayed daily the much longer "Eighteen." Knowing more about the central prayer of

Jesus' day, and the Lord's Prayer as the summary of it, can give us wisdom about how we should pray.

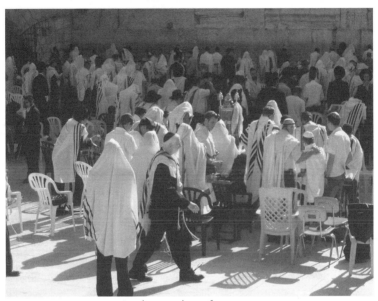

Jewish men gathering for prayer

The Amidah Prayer: A New Translation

It is important for Christians to be familiar with this central prayer of Jewish religious life. The prayer is very ancient, some of the changes to it being made 200 years before the time of Jesus. The prayer is also very beautiful, full of scriptural quotations and allusions.

The headings (e.g., "The God of History") that summarize each benediction or blessing are for reference only, and are not to be recited. The characterizations of God, which always follow ("Blessed are you, O Lord"), also can be used to summarize each benediction, and, if strung together, comprise a nice description of God.

The *Amidah*

1. The God of History:

Blessed are you, O Lord our God and God of our fathers, the God of Abraham, the God of Isaac and the God of Jacob, the great, mighty and revered God, the Most High God who bestows lovingkindnesses, the creator of all things, who remembers the good deeds of the patriarchs and in love will bring a redeemer to their children's children for his name's sake. O king, helper, savior and shield. Blessed are you, O Lord, the shield of Abraham.

2. The God of Nature:

You, O Lord, are mighty forever, you revive the dead, you have the power to save. [From the end of Sukkot until the eve of Passover, insert: You cause the wind to blow and the rain to fall.] You sustain the living with lovingkindness, you revive the dead with great mercy, you support the falling, heal the sick, set free the bound and keep faith with those who sleep in the dust. Who is like you, O doer of mighty acts? Who resembles you, a king who puts to death and restores to life, and causes salvation to flourish? And you are certain to revive the dead. Blessed are you, O Lord, who revives the dead.

3. Sanctification of God:

[Reader] We will sanctify your name in this world just as it is sanctified in the highest heavens, as it is written by your prophet: "And they call out to one another and say:
[Cong.] 'Holy, holy, holy is the LORD of hosts; the whole earth is full of his glory.'" [Is 6:3]
[Reader] Those facing them praise God saying:
[Cong.] "Blessed be the Presence of the LORD in his place." [Ezek 3:12]
[Reader] And in your Holy Words it is written, saying,
[Cong.] "The LORD reigns forever, your God, O Zion, throughout all generations. Hallelujah." [Ps 146:10]
[Reader] Throughout all generations we will declare your greatness, and to all eternity we will proclaim your holiness. Your praise, O our God, shall never depart from our mouth, for you are

a great and holy God and King. Blessed are you, O Lord, the holy God. You are holy, and your name is holy, and holy beings praise you daily. (Selah.) Blessed are you, O Lord, the holy God.

4. Prayer for Understanding:

You favor men with knowledge, and teach mortals understanding. O favor us with the knowledge, the understanding and the insight that come from you. Blessed are you, O Lord, the gracious giver of knowledge.

5. For Repentance:

Bring us back, O our father, to your Instruction; draw us near, O our King, to your service; and cause us to return to you in perfect repentance. Blessed are you, O Lord, who delights in repentance.

6. For Forgiveness:

Forgive us, O our Father, for we have sinned; pardon us, O our King, for we have transgressed; for you pardon and forgive. Blessed are you, O Lord, who is merciful and always ready to forgive.

7. For Deliverance from Affliction:

Look upon our affliction and plead our cause, and redeem us speedily for your name's sake, for you are a mighty redeemer. Blessed are you, O Lord, the redeemer of Israel.

8. For Healing:

Heal us, O Lord, and we will be healed; save us and we will be saved, for you are our praise. O grant a perfect healing to all our ailments, for you, Almighty King, are a faithful and merciful healer. Blessed are you, O Lord, the healer of the sick of his people Israel.

9. For Deliverance from Want:

Bless this year for us, O Lord our God, together with all the varieties of its produce, for our welfare. Bestow ([from the 15th of

Nissan insert:] dew and rain for) a blessing upon the face of the earth. O satisfy us with your goodness, and bless our year like the best of years. Blessed are you, O Lord, who blesses the years.

10. For Gathering of Exiles:

Sound the great shofar for our freedom, raise the ensign to gather our exiles, and gather us from the four corners of the earth. Blessed are you, O Lord, who gathers the dispersed of his people Israel.

11. For the Righteousness of God:

Restore our judges as in former times, and our counselors as at the beginning; and remove from us sorrow and sighing. Reign over us, you alone, O Lord, with lovingkindness and compassion, and clear us in judgment. Blessed are you, O Lord, the King who loves righteousness and justice.

12. For the Destruction of the Apostates and the Enemies of God:

Let there be no hope for slanderers, and let all wickedness perish in an instant. May all your enemies quickly be cut down, and may you soon in our day uproot, crush, cast down and humble the dominion of arrogance. Blessed are you, O Lord, who smashes enemies and humbles the arrogant.[4]

13. For the Righteous and Proselytes:

May your compassion be stirred, O Lord our God, towards the righteous, the pious, the elders of your people the house of Israel, the remnant of their scholars, towards proselytes, and towards us also. Grant a good reward to all who truly trust in your name. Set our lot with them forever so that we may never be put to shame, for we have put our trust in you. Blessed are you, O Lord, the support and stay of the righteous.

14. For the Rebuilding of Jerusalem:

Return in mercy to Jerusalem your city, and dwell in it as you have promised. Rebuild it soon in our day as an eternal structure, and quickly set up in it the throne of David. Blessed are you, O

Lord, who rebuilds Jerusalem.

15. For the Messianic King:

Speedily cause the offspring of your servant David to flourish, and let him be exalted by your saving power, for we wait all day long for your salvation. Blessed are you, O Lord, who causes salvation to flourish.

16. For the Answering of Prayer:

Hear our voice, O Lord our God; spare us and have pity on us. Accept our prayer in mercy and with favor, for you are a God who hears prayers and supplications. O our King, do not turn us away from your presence empty-handed, for you hear the prayers of your people Israel with compassion. Blessed are you, O Lord, who hears prayer.

17. For Restoration of Temple Service:

Be pleased, O Lord our God, with your people Israel and with their prayers. Restore the service to the inner sanctuary of your Temple, and receive in love and with favor both the fire-offerings of Israel and their prayers. May the worship of your people Israel always be acceptable to you. And let our eyes behold your return in mercy to Zion. Blessed are you, O Lord, who restores his divine presence to Zion.

18. Thanksgiving for God's Unfailing Mercies:

We give thanks to you that you are the Lord our God and the God of our fathers forever and ever. Through every generation you have been the rock of our lives, the shield of our salvation. We will give you thanks and declare your praise for our lives that are committed into your hands, for our souls that are entrusted to you, for your miracles that are daily with us, and for your wonders and your benefits that are with us at all times, evening, morning and noon. O beneficent one, your mercies never fail; O merciful one, your lovingkindnesses never cease. We have always put our hope in you. For all these acts may your name be blessed and exalted continually, O our King, forever and ever. Let every living thing give thanks to you and praise your name in truth, O God, our salvation and our help. (Selah.) Blessed are you, O Lord, whose Name is the Beneficent One, and to whom it is fitting to give thanks.

19. For Peace:

Grant peace, welfare, blessing, grace, lovingkindness and mercy to us and to all Israel, your people. Bless us, O our Father, one and all, with the light of your countenance; for by the light of your countenance you have given us, O Lord our God, a Torah of life, lovingkindness and salvation, blessing, mercy, life and peace. May it please you to bless your people Israel at all times and in every hour with your peace. Blessed are you, O Lord, who blesses his people Israel with peace.

---

[1] Rabban Gamaliel said: "One must say the Eighteen every day" (m. Berachot 4:3.

[2] Rabbi Yehoshua (m. Berachot 4:4).

[3] B. Berachot 29b.

[4] This nineteenth benediction (although twelfth in order) is called the "*Birkat HaMinim*" (Benediction of the Heretics) and was added approximately 60 to 70 years after the time of Jesus. It may have been a product of the mutual hostility between Jews and the growing movement of followers of Jesus.

"The Jewish Prayers of Jesus" was adapted and abridged from two articles by David Bivin: "Prayers for Emergencies," available at www.JerusalemPerspective.com; and "The Amidah Prayer: A New Translation," originally published electronically in *Jerusalem Perspective Pipeline*, now available at www.egrc.net.

10.

Why Didn't Jesus Get Married?

For thousands of years, Jesus' singleness has been a source of debate over how he expects the leaders of the church to live. Should we assume that singleness is his highest goal for followers who want to be like him? Looking at the lifestyle of rabbinic teachers of his day can shed some light on the issue.

The commandment "Be fruitful and multiply" (Gen 1:28) has always been strongly emphasized in Judaism, both today and in the first century. It is therefore surprising that Jesus, who in every other way observed the commandments, did not marry — at least the New Testament gives no indication that he had a wife or children.[1]

The rabbis taught that one should perpetuate the human race by marrying. It was considered especially significant that the commandment, "be fruitful and multiply," is chronologically the first in the Pentateuch. The school of Hillel ruled that to fulfill this commandment a man must have at least one son and one daughter:

> No man may neglect the commandment "Be fruitful and multiply" [Gen 1:28] unless he already has children: according to the school of Shammai, two sons; according to the school of Hillel, a son and a daughter, as it is written, "Male and female created he them." [Gen 1:27][2]

Would the members of first-century Jewish society have respected an unmarried 30-year-old teacher? Would his teaching have been given a hearing?

A bachelor rabbi functioning within Jewish society of the first century was not as abnormal as it might first appear. Rabbis often spent many years far from home, first as students and then as itinerant teachers. It was not uncommon for such men to marry in their late thirties or forties. Just as some students today wait to marry until they finish their education, so there were disciples and even rabbis who postponed marriage until later in life.

One such rabbi was Rabban Gamaliel, the grandson of Rabban Gamaliel the Elder, the apostle Paul's teacher (Acts 22:3; 5:34). As the following story shows, the younger Gamaliel was already a rabbi and already had disciples before he married:

> A bridegroom is exempt from reciting the Shema on the first night of his marriage.... When Rabban Gamaliel married he recited the Shema on the first night. His disciples said to him: "Master, didn't you teach us that a bridegroom is exempt from reciting the Shema on the first night?"
>
> "I will not listen to you," he replied, "so as to cast off from myself the Kingdom of Heaven even for a moment."[3]

Enamored with Torah

Another unmarried rabbi was Shim'on ben Azzai. He lived in the generation immediately after the destruction of the temple in A.D. 70. It is related of him that in his teaching he so strongly emphasized the importance of the commandment to marry, his colleagues expressed their amazement that he did not do so himself. His answer:

> What shall I do? I am enamored with Torah. Others can enable the world to continue to exist.[4]

So we see that it would have been possible for Jesus to have been accepted as a teacher in first-century Jewish society without his being married.

Although Shim'on ben Azzai was not married, he did not endorse the unmarried state. He may have married later in life. Jesus may not have been making a statement about the undesirability of marriage because of his unmarried state either. He was still relatively young when he was crucified, and his death may have come before he would have had a chance to marry.

---

[1] Michael Hilton and Gordian Marshall point out that the silence of the

Gospels might suggest that Jesus was married: "It was so unusual for rabbis not to marry that such a fact [Jesus had not married] would probably have been mentioned. Thus a Jew reading the Gospels might assume that Jesus was married" (*The Gospels and Rabbinic Judaism: A Study Guide* [Hoboken, NJ: Ktav, 1988], p. 135).

[2] M. Yevamot 6:6; cf. b. Yevamot 64a.

[3] M. Berachot 2:5. (The Shema was said twice daily by Jews in Jesus' time as a recommitment of one's self to the one true God of Israel. The statement "to cast off the Kingdom of Heaven" means to exempt oneself from God's reign. Even if the rabbi had one moment in all of his life that he was excused from submitting to God as his Lord, he still would not take it.)

[4] T. Yevamot 8:7.

"Why Didn't Jesus Get Married?" was adapted and abridged from the article, "Jesus, a Jewish Bachelor?" by David Bivin, which is available at www.JerusalemPerspective.com.

11.

Miracle on the Sea of Galilee

He [Jesus] got into one of the boats, the one belonging to Simon, and asked him to push out a little from the shore. Then he sat down and taught the people from the boat. When he had finished speaking, he said to Simon, "Push out into deep water and let down your nets for a catch." Simon answered, "Teacher, we have worked all night and caught nothing! However, if you say so, I will let down the nets." When they had done this, they enclosed a great school of fish ... when Simon Peter saw it, he fell at Jesus' feet and said, "Go away from me, Lord. I am a sinful man!" (Lk 5:3–6, 8)

Understanding more about ancient fishing on the Sea of Galilee allows us to paint, in vivid detail, this scene of one of the first miracles of Jesus' ministry as it occurred, likely during winter on the lake shore at Heptapegon near Capernaum.[1]

Peter and the other fishermen were using a trammel net to catch musht (*Tilapia galilea*; "St. Peter's fish"). They fished at night and stopped their work at dawn because in the light of day the fish could see the netting. Before the fishermen turned in for the day, they carefully washed their nets and hung them to dry. If the linen nets were not dried promptly after use they would rot in a short time. From the gospel account we learn that Jesus arrived at the lakeshore while the fishermen were still washing their nets, and immediately got into

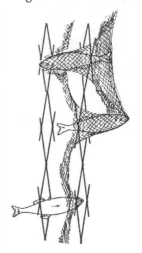

How fish are enmeshed in a layered trammel net

one of the boats and began to teach. If the washing of the trammel nets took place shortly after dawn, then Jesus must have begun teaching very early in the morning.[2]

Jewish sources support this picture of the diligence and faithfulness of teachers in Israel during this period, and the people's eagerness to learn Torah. From rabbinic literature one learns that the rabbis taught in every conceivable venue and at any time of the day or night. Here we have an example of a rabbi teaching in the early morning, perhaps as early as 7:00, from a boat moored offshore. A crowd large enough to cause Jesus to use a boat as a teaching platform had gathered, despite the early hour.

The Tough Work of the Fisherman

Was it just by chance that Jesus chose fishermen as disciples, or had their difficult work especially prepared them for the task for which they were chosen? The Sea of Galilee fishermen were tough. Their bodies were wet much of the time, even in the winter, for it is during the winter when fishing is at its best on the Sea of Galilee — the musht season is in the winter, as is the sardine season. The winter is also the rainy season in Israel, and it often rained on the fishermen during those long winter nights when they were out on the lake.[3] (In those days there were no rubberized rain gear like today's fishermen wear!)

The fisherman's work was also difficult physically, entailing rowing to and from the fishing sites, hauling in heavy nets and

A cast-net fisherman working from shore

lifting catches of fish. Cast-net fishermen had to dive under the water repeatedly to retrieve their nets. Most fishermen worked all night and slept during the day. We can image that a typical fishing village like Capernaum was quiet until 12:30 or 1:00 p.m., with mothers shushing noisy children or any dog that barked.

Put yourself in Peter's place, having worked all night in a small boat, in the cold, in the dark, perhaps in the rain. How would you feel if while washing your nets shortly after dawn, dead tired after a long night of fishing, someone climbed into your boat and asked you to row him out into the lake, and then you had to sit in the boat waiting for several hours while that person spoke to an audience? Before long, your patience would be wearing thin because you would not only be sleepy, you would begin to be very hungry as well. Imagine then being ordered to go back to work, to let down your nets again — after they had already been washed! What *chutzpah* on the part of Jesus!

Where was Jesus when he said to Peter, "Push out into the deep water and let down your nets for a catch?" Where was Jesus when Peter fell at his feet in shock and amazement? Our impression of the story in Luke 5:1-11 is sometimes colored by a similar story found in John 21:1-14. We often unconsciously harmonize these accounts even though the story in John takes place after the resurrection. We picture Jesus standing elegantly on the beach, perhaps with an arm outstretched towards Peter's boat some

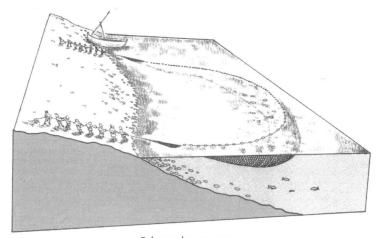

Fishing with a seine net

distance offshore. We envision Peter jumping out of his boat, swimming ashore, falling on his face on the beach before Jesus, and then climbing back aboard his boat to drag the loaded net ashore. This is due to the influence of John's account which has Peter, when he heard that it was the Lord, jumping out of his boat which was 200 cubits (about 90 meters) from land and swimming ashore.

However, in Luke's story, Jesus is in Peter's boat when he tells Peter to push out into the deep water and begin fishing again. Jesus also is in the boat when Peter falls at his feet immediately after the loaded fish nets are hauled into the boat.

It may seem to us from English translations of this story that Peter alone maneuvered the boat into position for Jesus' teaching session, that Peter alone took his boat out to deeper water, and that Peter single-handedly let down the nets. But Jesus' command — "Push out [plural] into the deep water and let down [plural] your [plural] nets for a catch" — indicates that there was at least one other fisherman from Peter's crew who got into the boat with Peter and Jesus. Also the statement in verse 7, "they motioned to their partners in the other boat to come and help them," shows that Peter was not the only fisherman in the boat.

The size and shape of trammel net boats have remained constant since the time of Jesus.

The crew is a minimum of two.

The trammel net boat was normally manned by four fishermen. It is therefore likely that there were two or three other fishermen who got into the boat along with Peter. (The trammel net boat could with some difficulty be operated by a crew of two — one crew member rowing and the other playing out and hauling in the nets.) If only two persons besides Peter and Jesus got into the boat, then perhaps Jesus served as the crew's fourth member. If three got in then Jesus was in the way, since in a boat of this size — fifteen to eighteen feet long — there was barely room for four fishermen, their nets and other equipment.

This alters the usual picture we have of Jesus' lakeside teaching session: as the crowd listened to Jesus, they saw him in a boat flanked by two to four fishermen. Furthermore, we have to picture Jesus, as the nets were being hauled into the boat, crowded into a corner of the boat and partially covered with nets and fish – unless he had replaced the fourth crew member and was helping to pull in the nets. Had Jesus himself spent time fishing on the Sea of Galilee?

The Miracle of the Catch

When Peter saw the enormous catch, he fell down in the boat in front of Jesus crying, "Go away from me, Lord. I am a sinful man!" The text adds that Peter and those with him were astonished "at the catch of fish which they had taken." Did these fishermen react this way because statistically it was unlikely that they would catch fish, not to speak of a near-record catch, after having worked all night and caught nothing? Yes, this partially accounts for their shock. The unlikelihood of now catching enough fish to be worth their while financially is also indicated by Peter's initial response. He didn't immediately do as Jesus said, but first argued a little: "Lord, we have worked all night and caught nothing."

But there is more to these Galilean fishermen's reaction of amazement than the catch itself or its size. Until the introduction of transparent nylon nets in the mid-1950s, trammel net fishing was done only at night. In the daytime, the fish could see the nets and avoid them. The miracle was that the fish swam blindly into the net. In addition, in trammel net fishing the fish had to be scared into the nets after the nets had been put in place. Although possible, it does not seem from Luke's account that the fishermen made a commotion to frighten the fish.

What was it, then, that caused Peter to fall in fear at Jesus' feet? Apparently, it was the timing of the miracle. It was amazement at Jesus' ability to, as we say, "call the shots." Immediately after he finished preaching, when it was convenient for him, Jesus compensated these fishermen for their inconvenience.

The confidence of Jesus stands out. To teach a crowd of people Jesus apparently did not mind the inconvenience he caused these fishermen because he planned to reward them for their service and knew that he could do so whenever he wished. We see this same confidence demonstrated by Peter after Pentecost when Peter, knowing in advance what he was going to do and what would be the result, healed a lifelong cripple (Acts 3:6).

Jesus was not unaware of the tiredness of the fishermen and their frustration at not having caught anything after working so hard all night. He knew that they were dead tired and wanted to go home and go to sleep. He also knew of their general need for income and their particular lack of it after this unsuccessful night of fishing. He removed their frustration at having wasted a night's work and blessed them with enough fish to compensate them not just for the few hours he took of their time but with as many fish as they would normally have caught in several nights of good fishing. The catch described in Luke 5 was about three-fourths of a ton — as much as a trammel net fishing crew would normally take in two week's work, allowing for nights like the one that Peter and his crew had just experienced when nothing is caught.

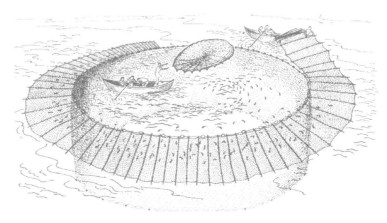

Another type of fishing using the veranda net. Fish try to escape the cylindrical trammel by jumping over it, but they land on the *veranda*.

[1] This chapter is based on the research of Mendel Nun, 87, who has spent a lifetime studying the ancient fishing methods used on the Sea of Galilee. Since Jesus spent so much time on or near the sea, and his first disciples were Sea of Galilee fishermen, Nun's work is important in illuminating many gospel stories.

[2] Nun also has shown that in the story of the miraculous catch, Peter could only have been using a trammel net or a veranda net, a variation of the trammel net. He could not have been fishing with a seine because it was not used near Heptapegon/Capernaum. The floor of the lake in that area of the coast is so rocky that the seine would have continually gotten hung up on the rocks. And it is unlikely that Peter was using a cast-net because he was fishing with a boat and crew.

[3] For more on trammel net fishing on the Sea of Galilee, see "Let Down Your Nets" by Mendel Nun, *Jerusalem Perspective* 24 (Jan/Feb 1990), pp. 11–13.

"Miracle on the Sea of Galilee" was adapted and abridged from the article, "The Miraculous Catch (Luke 5:1–11): Reflections on the Research of Mendel Nun," by David Bivin, which is available online at www.JerusalemPerspective.com.

III.

New Light on Jesus' Teachings

12.

The Rich Man Who Rejected the Kingdom

And behold, one came up to him, saying, "Teacher, what good deed must I do, to have eternal life?" And he said to him, "Why do you ask me about what is good? One there is who is good. If you would enter life, keep the commandments." ... The young man said to him, "All these I have observed; what do I still lack?" Jesus said to him, "If you would be perfect, go, sell what you possess and give to the poor, and you will have treasure in heaven; and come, follow me." When the young man heard this he went away sorrowful; for he had great possessions. (Mt 19:16–17, 20–22; RSV)

What Was the Rich Man's Question?

It can be conjectured that "What good can I do to inherit internal life?" was a question that was asked in first-century Israel. The question contains a clear reference to a question implied in Micah 6:8, "He has told you, O man, what [is] good, and what the LORD requires of you...." Although there is no confirmation in rabbinic sources, we may assume that there were rabbis who abbreviated Micah 6:8 and turned it into a question: "What good does the LORD require of you?" Apparently, there were others, like the rich man, who held a misguided, popular understanding of this shortened form of Micah 6:8, and asked, "What *mitzvah* (good deed; literally, commandment) can I do to obtain eternal life?"

Jesus responded, "Why do you say 'good'?" It is probable that Jesus was not questioning the rich man about what he meant when he used the word "good."[1] Jesus knew what he meant, but criticized him for the way he used "good." In this context, "Why do you say 'good'?" must mean, "Why do you use 'good' in this way?" The use of *amar* (to say) in the sense of "interpret" is common in rabbinic literature.[2]

Jesus strongly opposed the rich man's suggestion that eternal life could be procured by performing a good deed. Jesus agreed with other contemporary Jewish teachers that there exists a statement in Scripture that is so comprehensive that it summarizes all the commandments;[3] however, he opposed the idea that there are levels or grades of *mitzvot*. Jesus, like many contemporary rabbis, taught that "light" commandments are as important as "heavy" commandments (Mt 5:19).[4] In his view, care must be taken to observe even the most insignificant of God's commandments. Therefore, there cannot be one commandment, one "good deed," that opens the door to eternal life.

The doing of good deeds to obtain a reward was opposed not just by Jesus, but by most rabbis. The Midrash expounds it this way:

David said, "Some trust in their fair and upright deeds, and some in the works of their fathers, but I trust in you. Although I have no good works, yet because I call upon you, you answer me."[5]

The Pharisees criticized those of their number who continually asked, "What good deed may I do?" They caricatured themselves by speaking of seven types of Pharisees, and the fifth type was the "Calculating Pharisee" who was always saying, "Tell me what good deed I can do to offset a bad deed."[6]

One should also compare such rabbinic sayings as the following:

"Blessed is the man that delights greatly in his commandments" (Ps 112:1) — in his commandments, not in the reward of his commandments.[7]

Do not be like slaves who serve their master to receive a reward; rather, be like slaves who do not serve their master to receive a reward.[8]

In the rich man story, Jesus strongly emphasizes the importance of the *mitzvot*. However, Jesus expected his disciples to do good deeds out of love for God and a desire to please him, not to gain a reward — even the reward of eternal life. According to Jesus, when one has performed all the commandments, one has done no more than one's duty and is still just an undeserving slave, not having earned any reward:

> Would any of you, if you had a slave plowing or tending the sheep, say to him when he comes in from the field, "Come in and recline to eat"? No, you would say to him, "Prepare something for me to eat, then change your clothes and serve me until I have finished eating; after that, you may eat." So you too, when you have done all the things you are commanded, say, "We are unworthy slaves. We have only done what it was our duty to do." (Lk 17:7-8, 10)

This also is the view of Hillel and Shammai:

> If you have performed many *mitzvot* [literally, If you have done much Torah], do not think that you have any merit [i.e., that you are entitled to a reward]. This is the purpose for which you have been created![9]

The Ruler's Inner Unrest

The ruler was very rich, as Luke 18:23 tells us, and very observant. As an observant Jew of the first century, he undoubtedly already gave heavily to the poor. However, he wished to do something out of the ordinary, a deed that would assure him eternal life.

It is likely that Jesus' teaching had stirred the man. His question implies an inner unrest. Although he kept the commandments, and therefore Written and Oral Torah promised him eternal life, he desired to be sure that he would obtain it. Being rich, the man probably imagined that Jesus would command him to give a significantly large donation to the poor. Instead, Jesus admonished him, indicating that he should have a more balanced approach to Torah.

The man persisted in his almost flippant attitude toward Torah. He insisted impatiently: "You still have not given me an answer. I already keep these commandments." It was at this point that Jesus presented the rich man with a test that would reveal to the man and to everyone else how sincere he was in his desire for eternal life.

The rich man was shocked. He had not imagined that the rabbi would ask him to give up his entire fortune. His face fell, and he asked no further questions. Jesus used this situation, the rich man's negative response, to teach his disciples some important spiritual truths, such as the extreme difficulty the rich had in becoming his disciples.

Peter, like King David, was a man "after God's own heart." Peter was impetuous, but he always tried hard to please Jesus, and he was Jesus' most trusted disciple. Now, witnessing this dramatic exchange between Jesus and the rich man, Peter wanted to say or do something that would match the occasion. Peter could not claim that he and the other disciples had divested themselves of all their possessions, but they had joined Jesus' kingdom of disciples. So he stated that they had "left" everything, that is, they had temporarily given up family and possessions to follow Jesus.

Jesus did not put Peter down by reminding him that he had not made the sacrifice demanded of the rich man — "look here, you haven't given away everything." Rather, he tenderly affirmed Peter's declaration: Yes, that is wonderful. You, my dear disciples, made the sacrifices I demanded of you, and I know that you are still ready to make any sacrifices I ask of you, including the giving away of all your wealth. Therefore, I want you to know that anyone who leaves his family and livelihood for me, will, in the here and now, receive a blessing that will more than compensate for what he has given up; and, of course, he will also receive eternal life."

Learning from the Story of the Young Ruler

- One must serve God out of love, in order to please him, rather than to gain a reward. The rich man was looking for a reward.

- God will probably test our commitment to him at its weakest, most vulnerable point or points, those areas in our lives that we have made more important than him. The weakest link in the rich man's commitment to God was his love of possessions. Therefore, he was asked to give up his possessions. God probably will test us in a similar way. He will do this for our good, to strengthen areas of weakness in our lives that prevent us from reaching spiritual maturity.

- We must relearn the lesson of giving to those in need. The rich man was told that he would have treasure in heaven if he distributed his wealth to the poor. Let us not forget Jesus' teaching about giving with a "good eye" (Mt 6:22), that is, giving generously. If we do this, he promised that we would be full of God's light, or Holy Spirit.

- The Rich Young Ruler story illustrates the insidious nature of wealth and the grave spiritual danger it presents. (And we shouldn't suppose that a great deal of money is required to turn our thoughts from God. One can be just as stingy with a small sum as the rich sometimes are with their millions.) The rich man had become so attached to his possessions that he could not follow Jesus. On another occasion, Jesus warned that there are few who find the narrow gate and the straight way. The love of money is an extra weight that makes finding "life" just that much more difficult.

- We must count nothing more important than being Jesus' disciple. Jesus likened being part of the "Kingdom of Heaven," his band of disciples, to possessing a great treasure.

- Jesus promised that those who make sacrifices for his sake will receive "much more" in this life. We can take courage from that promise: the happiness we will experience, not just in the next life, but even in this life, will far outweigh the sacrifices we make to follow Jesus.

---

[1] Most likely, the Hebrew underneath *oudeis agathos ei me heis* (No one is good except one) originally referred to the Torah and not to God. Out of context, it might be plausible to assume that the word *heis* (one) refers to God, for God is called "good" in Scripture, and references to God such as *hatov vehametiv* (the Good and the Doer of Good) occur frequently in ancient Jewish prayers and blessings. In this context, however, it is almost impossible to suppose that the reference is to God, for Jesus immediately goes on to mention the commandments of Torah.

Supporting this idea is the fact that the word *heis* (one) here appears within the framework of the declaration *oudeis agathos ei me heis* (There is no one good except one), whose structure is so strikingly similar to the rabbinic saying *en tov ela torah* (There is no good except

Torah). It is difficult to imagine that here *heis* (one) could refer to anything but Torah.

[2] Especially when two sages disagree about the interpretation of a passage of Scripture: *...hu omer...va ani omer...* ("He says...and I say...," that is, "He interprets [as follows]...but my interpretation is....") (t. Sotah 6:6–11; Sifre Deuteronomy 31; to 6:4 [ed. Finkelstein, pp. 49–51]; Rosh ha-Shanah 18b, line 29). Compare the words of Jesus: "You have heard that it was said...but I say..." (Mt 5:21–22, 27–28, 33–34, 38–39, 43–44), that is, "You have heard such and such an interpretation of Scripture...but I differ with that interpretation. My interpretation is...."

[3] The sages referred to a comprehensive summary of Scripture as *kelal gadol batorah* (a great rule of Torah). Rabbi Akiva said that the most important summary statement in Scripture is, "You shall love your neighbor as yourself" (Sifra, Kedoshim; to Lev 19:18 [ed. Weiss, p. 89b]). Compare Luke 10:27, and parallels.

[4] This approach is known by its abbreviation, *kalah kahamurah* (light as heavy, i.e., a light [commandment is as important] as a heavy [commandment]). According to this approach, the less serious commandments are no less significant than the serious commandments. (See m. Avot 2:1, "Be as careful of a 'light' commandment as of a 'heavy' commandment, because you do not know the reward of each commandment.") See pp. 96–97 for more on this rabbinic practice.

[5] Midrash Psalms 141 (ed. Buber, pp. 530–31).

[6] J. Berachot IX, 14b; b. Sotah 22b; Avot de-Rabbi Natan, Version A, Chpt. 37 (ed. Schechter, p. 109); Version B, Chpt. 45 (p. 124).

[7] B. Avodah Zarah 19a.

[8] In other words, we should serve God out of love. This saying, preserved in the Mishnah (m. Avot 1:3), was transmitted by Antigonus of Socho, a sage who lived at the beginning of the second century B.C. To the saying of Antigonus, compare the phrase found in Derech Eretz Rabbah 2:13 (ed. Higger, p. 284): *osin meahavah* (those who do [i.e., perform good deeds] out of love).

All these sayings about observing the commandments were given to a Jewish audience which had undertaken the covenant of the Torah. For the early church's ruling on Gentile observance of the Torah, see pp. 141–143.

[9] Avot de-Rabbi Natan, Version B, Ch. 31 (ed. Schechter, p. 66). Note the expression "to do Torah." For this expression, compare Mishnah, Avot 6:7, "Great is the Torah for it gives life to them that do it, in this world and in the world to come." In the New Testament, compare *poietes nomou* (an observer [literally, a doer] of law) in James 4:11, and *poiei ton vomon* (observes [literally, does] the law) in John 7:19.

Apparently, in the time of Jesus, the expression "do Torah" was a synonym for "do commandments." If so, we can conclude that "Torah" was a synonym for "commandments." This insight enables us to better understand Jesus' abrupt switch from "Torah" to "commandments" in his reply to the rich man: "There is no good except one [i.e., Torah]. You know the commandments...."

"The Rich Man Who Rejected the Kingdom" was adapted and abridged from "A Hebraic Nuance of *lego*," and "The Rich Young Ruler Story: Personal Application" by David Bivin, which are available at www.JerusalemPerspective.com; as well as excerpts from Bivin's "Jerusalem Synoptic Commentary Preview: The Rich Young Ruler Story," *Jerusalem Perspective* 38 & 39 (May–Aug 1993), pp. 25–26.

13.

Us and Them: Loving Both

Not too long ago scholars stood at a great disadvantage in their efforts to explain the background to Jesus' famous saying on love: [1]

> You have heard it said, "You shall love your neighbor, and hate your enemy." But I say to you, "Love your enemy, and pray for those who persecute you in order that you may be sons of your Father who is in heaven; for He causes His sun to rise on the evil and the good, and sends his rain on the righteous and the unrighteous." (Mt 5:43-45, NASB)

In the past scholars speculated that Jesus was responding to a well-known folk proverb. Ancient Romans regarded treating friends kindly and taking revenge on enemies as being admirable. For example, Sulla, the famous Roman military commander, who died in 78 B.C., was honored by a monument bearing the inscription, "None of my friends ever did me a kindness, and none of my enemies ever did me a wrong, without being fully requited."[2] Undoubtedly, the underlying concept of this inscription circulated in proverbial form among the diverse people groups of the Roman empire in various languages. But did some such proverbial saying inspire Jesus to respond with, "But I say to you, 'Love your enemy...'"?

The larger context of Jesus' saying includes Matthew 5:21-48. Six times in these twenty-seven verses Jesus used the phrase, "But I say to you," and each time he was offering his own distinctive interpretation on a specific verse from the Torah. One could suggest that Jesus' words represent a response not to a proverb, but to an exegetical tradition linked to a verse from the Torah. If so, one may find clues helpful for illuminating the exegetical background of Jesus' saying embedded in Second Temple-period Jewish literature.

With the discovery of the Dead Sea Scrolls, scholars benefited immensely from the infusion of new linguistic, comparative, archaeological and historical data into their research. Included among the scrolls written in Hebrew is the Manual of Discipline, which apparently functioned in some capacity as a manual for initiates entering the Dead Sea sect. In the opening paragraph of this scroll, one reads, "...in order to love all that He has chosen and to hate all that He has rejected" (1QS 1.3–4). Later in the same scroll, similar instructions are repeated:

> These are the norms of the Way...in these times regarding love and hate: an eternal but concealed hatred for the Men of the Pit! [The member of the Way, that is, the sect] shall leave them his property and labor, as a slave does his owner, and a poor man his oppressor; but he [the member] shall be a zealot for God's Law, waiting for the Day of Vengeance. (1QS 9.21–23)

The Essene Vow of Hatred

When describing the three main religious groups of his day — the Pharisees, Sadducees and Essenes — Josephus wrote that twice daily before their common meal, the Essenes swore an oath. That oath included a pledge "to hate forever the unjust and to fight together with the just" (War 2:139). Josephus' report about the Essenes concurs with the attitude that the Manual of Discipline reflects.

The Essenes of the Dead Sea sect essentially saw themselves as allied with God, and according to their teachings, God would one day vindicate them and destroy those not belonging to the sect. Therefore, the Essenes taught that one should love his fellow-sectarians (those allied with God), but hate those outside the community (those opposed to God). Interestingly, their enmity was to be concealed like the ill will of a slave toward his master. They viewed their status in the God-ordained system of this transitory world in terms of a slave who harbors hate against his master, but feels helpless to rebel against the institution of slavery.[3]

Ancient Jews regarded Leviticus 19:17–18 as an important

passage about love: "You shall not hate your brother in your heart...you shall not avenge nor bear any grudge against one of your own people, but love your neighbor (*re'a*) as yourself." The passage prohibits harboring enmity against "a brother" and taking vengeance or bearing a grudge against someone from one's "own people." The second verse adds the positive command to love a "*re'a*" as oneself.

These verses clearly state that hating a person from one's own people — an insider, co-religionist, or friend — is forbidden. Applying a reverse type of logic, one could also interpret these verses to imply that hating a person not from one's own people — an outsider, non-sectarian, or enemy — is permitted. To discourage such a reading of the passage, Jesus broadened his interpretation of *re'a* to include an enemy.

Reading Matthew 5:43–45 against the background of the exegetical trends and sectarian attitudes reflected in the Dead Sea Scrolls, one appreciates better the aim of Jesus' saying.[4] Jesus rejected the sectarian paradigm, which the Essenes had built upon, the idea that God was for the righteous, but against the wicked. By doing so, he undermined the Essene doctrine of hatred toward those outside the sect.

For Jesus, Leviticus 19:18 spoke not only about loving friends, neighbors and fellow-sectarians, but also about loving enemies. In this instance, Jesus placed the non-sectarian well within the pale of a *re'a*. Elsewhere, Jesus interpreted *re'a* to include the Samaritans, a scorned class of foreigners (cf. Lk 10:25–37).

Jesus found further support for his interpretation in the way that God acts within the physical universe. God does good to all people. He does not single out the unrighteous for darkness, nor the wicked for shortage of rain (Mt 5:45). Rather, God lavishes goodness, mercy and kindness on the righteous and the unrighteous, and it is this model of conduct that Jesus encouraged his disciples to emulate.

---

[1] Based on the article by Magen Broshi, "Hatred: An Essene Religious Principle and Its Christian Consequences," *Antikes Judentum und Frühes Christentum* (Berlin: Walter de Gruyter, 1999), pp. 245–252.

Abridged and adapted by David Bivin and Joseph Frankovic.

[2] The inscription has been quoted from Philip Van Ness Myers, *Rome: Its Rise and Fall*, 2nd ed. (Boston: Ginn and Company, 1901), p. 262.

[3] Krister Stendahl, "Hate, Non-Retaliation, and Love," *Harvard Theological Review* 55 (1962), pp. 343–355; David Flusser, *Judaism and the Origins Of Christianity* (Jerusalem: Magnes Press, 1988), pp. 483–489.

[4] Morton Smith was the first to point out the relationship between Matthew 5:43 and the Manual of Discipline. See Morton Smith, "Mt. 5:43: 'Hate Thine Enemy,'" *Harvard Theological Review* 45 (1952), pp. 71–73.

"Us and Them: Loving Both" was adapted from the article, "Us and Them: Loving Both," available at www.Jerusalem Perspective.com. That article was based on the article by Magen Broshi, "Hatred: An Essene Religious Principle and Its Christian Consequences," *Antikes Judentum und Frühes Christentum* (Berlin: Walter de Gruyter, 1999), pp. 245–252, which was abridged and adapted by David Bivin and Joseph Frankovic.

14.

Jesus' Technical Terms About the Law

Jesus was very much a part of the rabbinic dialogue of his day. The sages focused their discussions on the interpretation of the Torah in order to understand how God's word applied to their lives. Frequently Jesus employed the technical terminology that was traditionally used in these discussions, terminology that may not always be clear to us. Knowing more about rabbinic technical terms will clarify Jesus' words.

Destroying or Fulfilling the Law

Think not that I have come to abolish the law and the prophets; I have come not to abolish them but to fulfill them. (Mt 5:17, RSV)

Jesus' words about abolishing and fulfilling the law are a puzzle to most of us. Some Christian commentators have interpreted this verse as if the Law were lacking something, something that Jesus provided. Rather than being destroyed, they say, the Law reached its fulfillment in Jesus, the Messiah.

But if we take a new look at the passage in light of its rabbinic context, we get a different picture:

• The verse begins with the words "I have come." The Hebrew verb "to come" often is used idiomatically to denote intent or purpose. When Jesus said, "I have come," he may not have been referring to his Incarnation, but rather speaking of intent. The reader who takes the words, "I have come," literally, may imagine Jesus leaving his heavenly throne and coming down to earth. But it is much more likely that Jesus was using "come" idiomatically to mean, "my purpose is...."

- The King James Version translators rendered the following Greek phrase as "to destroy the law." However, the probable Hebrew equivalent of the Greek verb translated "to destroy" is *levatel* (literally, "to cancel"), which was used in scholarly rabbinic discussions of Jesus' day as a technical term for violating a biblical commandment.[1]

- The probable Hebrew equivalent of the Greek verb *plerosai*, translated "fulfill" in Matthew 5:17, is *lekayem*. In Jesus' time *lekayem* was usually the antonym of *levatel* (cancel, nullify) and used in the sense of "preserve" or "sustain." Here, as a rabbinic technical term, it means, "to sustain by properly interpreting."

When a rabbi felt that a colleague had misinterpreted a passage of Scripture, he would say, "You are canceling (or, uprooting) the Torah!"[2] In other words, "You are so misinterpreting Scripture that you are negating or canceling part of it." Needless to say, in most cases, his colleague disagreed. What was "canceling" the Torah for one teacher was "fulfilling" it for another.

What one encounters in Matthew 5:17–19 is a rabbinic debate. Apparently, someone had suggested that Jesus was "canceling" the Torah. He was politely accused of misinterpreting the Scriptures so as to nullify their intent. Jesus politely disagreed, using the usual technical terminology for such situations, the Hebrew verbs *levatel* and *lekayem*.

Not One Jot or Tittle

In the next verse, Matthew 5:18, Jesus employed hyperbole to show just how strongly he felt about the importance of Torah. Not a *yod*, the smallest letter of the Hebrew alphabet, nor even a *kots*, the tiny decorative spur sometimes added to the *yod*, would ever be removed from the Torah, he said.

The meaning of this exaggeration, *lo yod ve-lo kotso shel yod* (not a *yod* and not a *kots* of a *yod*), a well-known Hebrew expression, was, "not the most insignificant thing." When Jesus declared that heaven and earth might sooner disappear than the smallest letter of the Hebrew alphabet, or even its optional decorative stroke, he was saying in a very picturesque way that the

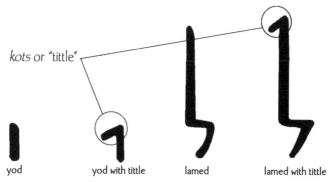

kots or "tittle"

yod   yod with tittle   lamed   lamed with tittle

The yod was usually written with a tiny horizontal line on the top left, an ornamental spur added to some Hebrew letters. This decoration was called a *kots*, which means "thorn." In Greek *kots* was translated by the word *keraia*, literally, "horn," which was in turn rendered *"tittle"* by the translators of the King James Version. In Jesus' day the *kots* was not horizontal, as in printed modern scripts, but angled down and to the left like a fishhook or the barb of a thorn – for this reason it was called a thorn in Hebrew.

Torah given by God to Moses would never cease to exist. Many rabbinic sayings express the same idea, such as the following:

Everything has an end — heaven and earth have an end — except one thing that has no end. And what is that? The Torah.[3]

No letter will ever be abolished from the Torah.[4]

Should all the nations of the world unite to uproot one word of the Torah, they would be unable to do it.[5]

Although Jesus spoke hyperbolically about letters and strokes being removed from the Torah, one should not think that he or any of his fellow rabbis believed that the Torah would not endure forever. From English versions of the New Testament one might get the impression that Jesus was being accused of intending to abolish or replace the Torah. However, when Matthew 5:17–19 is placed in its Hebraic and Jewish context, one understands that Jesus and his interlocutors were engaged in a typical rabbinic debate.

If we relate the Greek text of Matthew 5:17–18 to its Hebrew equivalents, and then translate those idioms to English, the following text results:

Do not suppose that I have any intention of undermining Scripture by misinterpreting it. My purpose is to establish and maintain the knowledge and observance of God's Word, not undermine it.[6]

Another way of bringing this saying into everyday English would be to render Jesus' words as, "I would not think of abrogating the Torah through misinterpretation. My intent is not to weaken or negate God's written Instruction, but to sustain and establish it by correct interpretation. I would never invalidate the Torah by effectively removing something from it through misinterpretation. Heaven and earth would sooner disappear than something from the Torah. Not the smallest letter in the alphabet, the *yod*, nor even its decorative spur, will ever disappear from the Torah."

The Importance of Light Commandments

Jesus went on to suggest (vs. 19) that one should not consider unimportant even the most seemingly insignificant commandments of the Torah.

> Whosoever therefore shall break one of these least commandments, and shall teach men so, he shall be called the least in the kingdom of heaven: but whosoever shall do and teach them, the same shall be called great in the kingdom of heaven. (Mt 5:19, KJV)

It is highly probable that in this context Jesus was speaking about *mitsvot kalot* (light commandments), which was a rabbinic technical term for biblical commandments of lesser importance. The opposite of *mitsvot kalot* was *mitsvot hamurot* (heavy or serious commandments), commandments of greater importance.

It is likewise probable that in Matthew 5:19 Jesus introduced a wordplay; he used the adjectives *kal* (light) and *hamur* (serious) to speak of people. In reference to people, the Hebrew words *kal* and *hamur* have the senses "insignificant, unimportant" and "significant, important," respectively.[7]

Obviously, a commandment is not absolutely "light" or "serious," but only so in comparison to other commandments. One commandment was so light, however, that it was often noted as such by the sages:

> If, along the road, you chance upon a bird's nest, in any tree or on the ground, with fledglings or eggs and the

mother sitting over the fledglings or on the eggs, do not take the mother together with her young. Let the mother go, and take only the young, in order that you may fare well and have a long life. (Deut 22:6-7; JPS)

The reward that God promised for not taking the mother bird with her young — a commandment that the sages called "the lightest of the light" (t. Shabbat 16:14) — is the same as for keeping the commandment, "Honor your father and your mother" (Ex 20:12; Deut 5:16), one of the Ten Commandments. The rabbis commented, "If, speaking of a light commandment, which deals with something that is worth only an *issar*,[8] the Torah has said, 'that it may be well with you and that you may prolong your days [Deut 22:7],' how much more [will the like reward be given] for [keeping] the weightier commandments of the Torah."[9]

The reason for being careful about keeping light commandments is that one does not know how God esteems the various commandments. The rabbis said, "Be as careful of [keeping] a light commandment as a heavy commandment because you do not know the reward given for the keeping of commandments."[10] This approach to Scripture caused one rabbi to say, "Woe unto us that Scripture gave the same weight to the light commandments as to the heavy commandments."[11]

Jesus adopted the same well-known rabbinic approach to the Torah: *kalah ka-hamurah* (light as heavy), an abbreviation of *mitsvah kalah ka-mitsvah hamurah* (a light commandment is as heavy as a heavy commandment), in other words, a light commandment is no less important than a heavy commandment.

Following his statement about the Torah in Matthew 5:17-20, Jesus gave five illustrations of this approach to the Torah (Mt 5:21-30, 33-48), in each juxtaposing two commandments, one heavy and one light.[12] For example, Jesus mentioned the command, "Do not murder," and then added, "But I say unto you, 'Do not hate your brother in your heart.'" In other words, according to Jesus' approach, to hate or be angry with someone was no less serious than to murder someone! Using similar logic, he made the sin of looking at a woman lustfully equivalent to committing adultery with her (Mt 5:27-28).

Employing the same approach, other rabbis said: "He who

violates a light command will ultimately violate a heavy one; he who violates, 'Love your neighbor as yourself [Lev 19:18],' will ultimately violate, 'You shall not hate your brother in your heart [Lev 19:17],' and 'You shall not take vengeance nor bear any grudge [Lev 19:18],' and even, 'He shall live with you' [Lev 25:35], until in the end he will come to shedding blood."[13]

Jesus taught that a disciple who abolished (i.e., misinterpreted) the light commandments, who did not do them, or who did not emphasize their importance when teaching, would be considered "light" in the "Kingdom of Heaven." A disciple who broke even a "light" commandment would be considered "light" (insignificant, unimportant) in Jesus' movement, which he called the "Kingdom of Heaven."

Binding and Loosing

And I will give unto thee the keys of the kingdom of heaven: and whatsoever thou shalt bind on earth shall be bound in heaven: and whatsoever thou shalt loose on earth shall be loosed in heaven. (Mt 16:19, KJV)

The Hebrew words for "bind" and "loose," *asar* and *hitir*, each appear with more than one meaning in the Hebrew Bible. "Bind" can mean "tie" as in Judges 15:12 and 16:11; "imprison" as in 2 Kings 17:4; "hitch" (a cart, wagon or chariot) as in Genesis 46:29; and "tether" as in Genesis 49:11; while *hitir* can be the exact opposite of *asar* in each of these senses.

By the time of Jesus, *asar* had acquired the additional meaning "forbid," and its antonym *hitir* had acquired the meaning "permit." These are the meanings most often found in rabbinic literature. The sages were called upon constantly by their community to interpret scriptural commands. The Bible forbids working on the Sabbath, for instance, but it does not define what constitutes work. As a result, the sages were required to rule on which activities were permitted on the Sabbath. They "bound," or prohibited, certain activities, and "loosed" or allowed, others.

The Mishnah contains many rabbinic rulings on what is "loosed" and what is "bound," such as the following:

During the war of Vespasian they [the rabbis] "bound" the

garlands of bridegrooms and the (playing of) bells [at weddings]. During the war of Quietus, they "bound" the garlands of brides and that no one should teach his son Greek. During the last war [the Bar-Kochba Revolt] they "bound" the bride's riding about the village in a litter.[14]

If a person made a vow to abstain from milk, he is "loosed" to eat whey. Rabbi Yose "binds" it... If a person made a vow to abstain from meat, he is "loosed" to eat broth [i.e., the water in which the meat was cooked]... Rabbi Yehudah "binds" it... If a person made a vow to abstain from wine, he is "loosed" to eat a cooked dish which has the taste of wine.[15]

The words in the Greek text of Matthew 16:19 that are translated "bind" and "loose" are forms of the verbs *dein* and *luein*. In the Septuagint *dein* is the usual Greek translation of the Hebrew *asar* while *luein* is twice the translation of *hitir*. In normal koine Greek, *dein's* range of meaning is similar to that of the earlier, biblical meaning of *asar* —"tie, bind, imprison," and *luein's* to that of *hitir*— "untie, loose, release from prison." None of these meanings seems to fit the context of Jesus' words to Peter.

It is possible that a Greek translator used forms of the Greek verbs *dein* and *luein* to translate *asar* and *hitir*, rather than trying to capture in a free translation the more recently acquired meanings of these Hebrew words. This would explain the odd way *dein* and *luein* are used in this context. The translator's choice of words would agree with the customary practice of using equivalents that had been fixed by generations of predecessors, rather than using dynamic equivalents. In other words, the Greek translator might have translated *asar* and *hitir* by their Septuagintal Greek equivalents even though in this passage *asar* and *hitir* had taken on the idiomatic sense of forbid and permit.

Jesus' movement was a new phenomenon in Jewish history, and he referred to it as the "Kingdom of Heaven." Situations soon would arise that none of the members of this movement had ever faced, and about which the Bible gave no specific instructions. Jesus, their teacher, would no longer be there to make the decisions, to say what was permitted and what was forbidden. It would be necessary for others to take Jesus' place.

Peter was given "the keys of the Kingdom of Heaven." Keys symbolize authority, as Isaiah indicates: "In that day I will summon my servant Eliakim...I will entrust him with your authority...I will place on his shoulders the keys to the house of David; what he unlocks no one may lock, and what he locks no one may unlock" (Is 22:20–24). Similarly, Jesus authorized Peter to find scriptural solutions for problems the early Church would encounter after Jesus' death. Peter was not to be indecisive, for Jesus had given him the authority to make rulings binding on the rest of his community, and had promised that "Heaven" would endorse his decisions: "Whatever you 'bind' on earth will be 'bound' in Heaven"— the decisions he made would have the authority of Heaven — in other words, they would be upheld by God, for "Heaven" was a common euphemism for God.

The leaders of the new movement, like other rabbis of this time, were called upon by their community to interpret Scripture, settle disputes and find answers in times of crisis. Sometimes they were compelled to deal with relatively minor conflicts such as the complaints of the Greek-speaking members of the community, who felt their widows were not being treated as well as the Hebrew-speaking widows (Acts 6:1–6). At other times these leaders were required to settle disputes of a more serious nature.

Acts 15 describes one such controversy: Should Gentiles be admitted into the fellowship without first being circumcised and obliged to keep the Torah of Moses? The decision reached is a classic example of how the leaders of the new community exercised their authority to "bind" and "loose."

The apostles and elders convened in Jerusalem, and after much discussion, Peter ruled that the yoke of the commandments was too heavy for Gentiles (Acts 15:10), that they should be "loosed" from the obligation to keep the Torah of Moses. James, Jesus' brother, concurred, but he "bound" as well as "loosed." He ruled that it was necessary for Gentiles who became members of Jesus' movement to distance themselves from idolatry, sexual immorality and murder (Acts 15:20), which in Jewish eyes were the universal biblical prohibitions, the minimal observance of Torah required of Gentiles.[16]

[1] For example, t. Sanhedrin 14:13: "He who prophesies to uproot *[la'akor]* a commandment of the Torah is culpable. Rabbi Simeon rules, 'If he prophesies to nullify *[levatel]* part and to keep *[lekayem]* part, he is not culpable. However, if his prophecy is to commit idolatry, even if he maintains *[lekayem]* it today and nullifies *[levatel]* it tomorrow, he is culpable.'" In this saying we see that *levatel* is the synonym of *la'akor*, and that their opposite is *lekayem*.

Here are a few of the occurrences in rabbinic literature of the use of *lekayem* in the sense of "interpret (or, apply) Scripture": "Papus said to him [to Rabbi Akiva], 'So how do you interpret *[lekayem]*, "The man has now become like one of us"'?" (Mechilta, Beshallah 6; to Gen 3:22); "Then to what do I apply *[lekayem]*, 'And you will eat it in haste'?" (Mechilta, Bo 7; to Ex 12:11); "How does Rabbi Lazar interpret *[lekayem]*, 'sons'? [in a discussion of Lev 21:5]" (j. Kiddushin 61c); "How do I interpret *[lekayem]*, 'The teacher sought to discover useful sayings' [Eccl 12:10]?" (j. Kiddushin 61c).

[2] When Rabbi Eliezer thought that Rabbi Akiva was suggesting in his interpretation that the slaughtering of the Passover lamb could not overrule the prohibition against work on Sabbath, although the Torah says it can, he said to Rabbi Akiva, "Akiva, you have uprooted *[la'akor]* what is written [in the Torah]" (m. Pesahim 6:2). In other words, "Akiva, you have overturned a scriptural command."

[3] Genesis Rabbah 10:1.

[4] Exodus Rabbah 6:1.

[5] Leviticus Rabbah 19:2.

[6] Below are the steps involved in moving from the Greek text to the conjectured Hebrew equivalent:

Greek (Nestle-Aland, 27th ed.):
Me nomisete hoti elthon katalusai ton nomon e tous prophetas. Ouk elthon katalusai alla plerosai.

Literal Translation of the Greek:
"Do not think that I came to destroy the law or the prophets. I did not come to destroy but to fill."

Conjectured Hebrew Reconstruction:
Al tahshevu she-bati levatel et ha-torah o et ha-nevi'im; lo bati levatel ela lekayem.

Literal Translation of the Conjectured Hebrew:
"Do not think that I have come to cancel the Torah [the five books of Moses] and the Prophets [the second section of the Hebrew canon]. I have not come to cancel but to sustain."

Dynamic Translation of the Conjectured Hebrew:

"Do not suppose that I have any intention of undermining Scripture by misinterpreting it. My purpose is to establish and maintain the knowledge and observance of God's Word, not undermine it."

[7] Compare Numbers Rabbah 8:3.

[8] The *issar* was a small copper coin whose purchasing power was approximately one half of a loaf of bread, about one twenty-fourth of a day's wage.

[9] M. Hullin 12:5.

[10] M. Avot 2:1.

[11] Rabban Yohanan ben Zakkai, b. Hagigah 5a.

[12] Matthew 5:21–26 is the first of five examples given by Jesus to illustrate his method of interpreting Scripture. The commandment, "Do not hate your brother in your heart" is found in Leviticus 19:17. The commandment, "Do not murder" is found in Exodus 20:13 and Deuteronomy 5:17.

[13] Sifre Deuteronomy, Shoftim 187.11.

[14] M. Sotah 9:14.

[15] M. Nedarim 6:5–7.

[16] See pp. 141–144 for more.

"Jesus' Technical Terms about the Law" was adapted and abridged from the following articles by David Bivin, which are available at www.JerusalemPerspective.com: "Matthew 5:17: 'Destroy' the Law," "Matthew 5:19: The Importance of 'Light' Commandments," and "'Binding' and 'Loosing.'"

15.

Jesus' View of Pacifism

The idea that Jesus taught pacifism arose primarily due to the misunderstanding of a number of his sayings. When viewed from a Jewish perspective, the gospel passages on which pacifism is based point to a quite different conclusion.

Many people over the years have seen Jesus as a pacifist — and for good reason. Here was a man who apparently was willing to die rather than defend himself, a man who taught his disciples not to kill, not to resist evil, to love their enemies, not to fear those who kill the body, and that only those who are willing to lose their lives will be able to save them.[1] Jesus' teachings seem very much like those of such popular pacifists as Tolstoy and Gandhi, and indeed, Tolstoy based his views on gospel passages.[2]

But did Jesus teach that it is wrong to defend oneself against attack? Did he really mean that we should not resist evil? Such a view seems to contradict what we read elsewhere in the Bible. In Romans 12:9, for example, Paul says that one should "hate what is evil," and in James 4:7 we read that we are to "resist the devil." It is clear from passages in Luke 22 that Jesus' disciples were armed,[3] and Jesus himself advised them to purchase swords.[4]

These apparent contradictions may be reconciled by recognizing the Hebraic nuances of the gospel texts, and by developing a deeper understanding of the Jewish background to Jesus' words.

Kill or Murder?

One verse that is commonly cited in support of Jesus' pacifism is Matthew 5:21, which most English versions of the Bible render, "You shall not kill." The Greek word translated "kill" in this passage is a form of the verb *phoneuo*. This verb was always used as the equivalent of the Hebrew verb *ratsah* in the Septuagint Greek translation of the Hebrew Scriptures. *Ratsah* is the word used in the sixth commandment in both Exodus 20:13 and its parallel, Deuteronomy 5:17. It seems quite certain that in Matthew 5:21 Jesus was quoting the sixth commandment.

The words *phoneuo* and *ratsah* are both ambiguous and can mean either "kill" or "murder," depending upon the context. However, God himself commanded capital punishment for such crimes as deliberate murder (Ex 21:12–15), rape (Deut 22:25–26), kidnapping (Ex 21:16), adultery (Lev 20:10; Deut 22:22), sorcery (Ex 22:18), and many other crimes. The sixth commandment, therefore, must be a prohibition against murder, not killing as such.

In spite of this, the King James Version of 1611, and the revisions of 1885 (Revised Version) and 1952 (Revised Standard Version), used "kill" rather than "murder" in translating Jesus' quotation of this commandment.[5] Although most recent translations of the Bible have corrected this mistake,[6] the use of "kill" in the King James Version and its successors has strongly influenced many English-speaking Christians' views of self-defense.

Another saying of Jesus on which his supposed pacifism is based is found in Matthew 5:39a. It is usually translated, "Do not resist evil," or "Do not resist one who is evil." However, when Jesus' saying is translated back into Hebrew, it is seen to be a quotation of a well-known Hebrew proverb that appears with slight variations in Psalms 37:1, 8 and Proverbs 24:19.[7]

This Hebrew maxim is usually translated, "Do not fret because of evildoers," or "Do not be vexed by evildoers." Bible translators apparently have supposed from the contexts of this maxim in Psalm 37 and Proverbs 24, which emphasize that evildoers will be destroyed, that the righteous should not be concerned about evildoers or pay them any attention. This supposition is strengthened by the second half of Psalms 37:1 that, as it is usually translated, advises that one should not be envious of such evildoers. It thus appears that the verb translated "fret" or "be vexed" is correctly translated. However, elsewhere in the Bible this verb always seems to have some sense of the meaning "anger."[8] Furthermore, the two parallels to this verb in Psalms 37:8, both synonyms for anger, suggest that the verb in Matthew 5 must also have that meaning.

The verb in question is from the root *h-r-h*, whose basic meaning is "burn." From this root meaning is derived "anger," a sense that all Hebrew words from this root have in common. (Note that in English also, many verbs expressing anger have something to do with fire or burning — be hot, burn, boil, flare up.) In some occurrences of this root, anger is a result of jealousy or rivalry. Saul's jealousy of David caused him to fly into a rage (1 Sam 20:7, 30). This nuance of *h-r-h* is also reflected in the use of "contend" in Isaiah 41:11: "Shamed and chagrined shall be all who contend with you" (JPS).

The particular form of the verb used in our proverb is a form for intensive action and thus expresses a passionate anger. This furious anger leads to a response in kind. Such anger results in a rivalry to see who can get the better of the other, and in each round of the competition the level of anger and violence rises. This amounts to responding to evil on its own terms, to competing in doing wrong with those who wrong us.

Do Not Try to Outdo Evildoers

The New English Bible's translation of Psalms 37:1 and 37:8 is unique: "Do not strive to outdo the evildoers or emulate those who do wrong. For like grass they soon wither and fade like the green of spring"; "Be angry no more, have done with wrath; strive not to outdo in evildoing." This seems to be the only version of the Bible that reflects the Hebrew "anger" verb's nuance of rivalry or competition.

Likewise, the Good News Bible is apparently the only translation of the New Testament that uses "revenge," or anything similar, to render Matthew 5:38–39:

> You have heard that it was said, "An eye for an eye, and a tooth for a tooth." But now I tell you: do not take revenge on someone who does you wrong. If anyone slaps you on the right cheek, let him slap your left cheek too.

It is surprising there are not other versions that translate in the same way. Following "But I tell you," the context demands "Do not take revenge," since the first part of verse 39 speaks of "an eye for an eye," in other words, punishment that is a response in kind.

In idiomatic English, Matthew 5:39a might read simply, "Don't try to get even with evildoers."[9] Not "competing" with evildoers is very different from not resisting evildoers. Jesus was not teaching that one should submit to evil, but that one should not seek revenge. Jesus' statement has nothing to do with confronting a murderer or facing an enemy on the field of battle. As Proverbs 24:29 says, "Do not say, 'I will do to him as he has done to me. I will pay the man back for what he has done.'"

English mistranslation of Matthew 5:39a has created a theological contradiction, but when Jesus' saying is correctly understood, it harmonizes beautifully with other New Testament passages:

> See that none of you pays back evil with evil; instead, always try to do good to each other and to all people. (1 Thess 5:15)

> Do not repay evil with evil or curses with curses, but with blessings. Bless in return — that is what you have been called to do — so that you may inherit a blessing. (1 Pet 3:9)

> Bless those who persecute you. Bless them, do not curse them. Do not pay anyone back with evil for evil.... If it is possible, as far as it depends on you, live peaceably with everyone. Beloved, do not take revenge, but leave that to the wrath of God. (Rom 12:14, 17–19)

Or, as Jesus commanded, "Love your enemies and pray for those who persecute you" (Mt 5:44). Our response to evil does have to be resistance — it is morally wrong to tolerate evil. However, we also must continue to show love for the evildoer.

It should be noted that loving and praying for one's enemies in no way precludes defending oneself when one's life is in danger. One is morally obligated to preserve life, including one's own. Jesus never taught that it is wrong to defend oneself against life-threatening attack. However, he consistently taught his disciples to forgive and not to seek revenge against those who had insulted or wronged them. As Proverbs 20:22 counsels, "Do not say, 'I will repay the evil deed in kind.' Trust in the LORD. He will take care of it." Our responsibility is not to respond in kind to offenses directed against us. That only prolongs and perpetuates the evil. We are not to "be overcome by evil," but to "overcome evil with good" (Rom 12:21).

Not only does a pacifistic interpretation of Jesus' sayings contradict many biblical passages, but pacifism was never a part of Jewish belief. According to Scripture, for example, a person who kills a housebreaker at night is not guilty of murder: "If a thief is seized while tunneling [to break into a house], and he is beaten to death, the person who killed him is not guilty of bloodshed" (Ex 22:2). The rationale is that the thief is ready to murder anyone who surprises him, thus one may preempt the thief.

The Jewish position on this issue is summed up in the rabbinic dictum, "If someone comes to murder you, anticipate him and kill him first."[10] The rabbis taught that if one is in danger of being murdered, he should defend himself, even if there is a measure of doubt about the intention of the attacker. Furthermore, if another person's life is threatened, one is obligated to prevent that murder, if necessary by killing the attacker.[11] The rabbis ruled that a person who is pursuing someone else with intent to murder may be killed.[12] In light of this, it is very unlikely that Jesus, a Jew of the first century, would have espoused pacifism.

When we examine Jesus' words from a Hebraic-Jewish perspective, we can see what has been obscured by mistranslation and lack of familiarity with Judaism. The passages construed to support pacifism actually condemn revenge rather than self-defense. It is not surprising that this interpretation is consistent with Jesus' other teachings and the rest of biblical instruction.

---

[1] Mt 5:21; 5:39a; 5:44; 10:28; 16:25.

[2] See Leo Tolstoy, *The Kingdom of God Is within You*, trans. Constance Garnett (New York, 1894; repr. Lincoln: University of Nebraska Press, 1984). In 1894 Mohandas Karamchand Gandhi, at that time a barrister in South Africa, read *The Kingdom of God Is within You*, which had been loaned to him by a Quaker. The book "overwhelmed" him, he wrote in his autobiography.

In 1906 Gandhi, struggling against racial prejudice in South Africa, launched a campaign of nonviolent civil disobedience. In 1910 he founded Tolstoy Farm for the families of men who were jailed in the struggle. Later, in India, Gandhi founded other such communities based on Tolstoy's ideology. In 1920 he proclaimed his program of nonviolent non-cooperation with the British rulers of India that led to freedom from British rule.

[3] Lk 22:38, 49.

[4] Lk 22:36.

[5] In addition to the King James Version and its revisions, such versions as the New Jerusalem Bible, The Living Bible and The Amplified Bible render Matthew 5:21 as "kill." However, The Living Bible and The Amplified Bible show inconsistency by translating the sixth commandment using "murder" (Ex 20:13; Deut 5:17).

[6] Rendering Matthew 5:21 by "murder" or "commit murder" are the New English Bible, New International Version, New American Standard Bible, New American Bible, Good News Bible, New Berkeley Version and the New Testament translations of Goodspeed, Moffatt, Phillips, Stern (Jewish New Testament) and Weymouth.

[7] I am indebted to Robert L. Lindsey for drawing my attention to the connection between Matthew 5:39a and these three passages. Psalm 37:1 and Proverbs 24:19 read *al tithar bamere'im* (Do not be furiously angry with evildoers). Psalm 37:8 reads *al tithar ach lehare'a* (Do not be furiously angry; it can only do harm).

[8] See the entry *harah* in *Theological Dictionary of the Old Testament*, ed. G. Johannes Botterweck and Helmer Ringgren (Grand Rapids: Eerdmans, 1986), 5:171–76.

[9] "Wrongdoers" might be preferable to "evildoers." As the context, which mentions insults and lawsuits, shows, Jesus probably was not speaking primarily of confrontations with criminals or enemies on the field of battle, but of confrontations with ordinary acquaintances who have committed an offense.

[10] B. Sanhedrin 72a.

[11] This ruling was based on Leviticus 19:16: "You must not stand idly by when your neighbor's life is at stake" (New English Translation).

[12] M. Sanhedrin 8:7.

"Jesus' View of Pacifism" was adapted and abridged from the article, "Jesus' View of Pacifism," by David Bivin, which is available online at www.JerusalemPerspective.com.

16.

Jesus' Attitude Toward Poverty

Certain circles within the Judaism of Jesus' day took the view that there was something spiritually beneficial in poverty per se, that it was a mark of God's special favor to be poor.[1] Given Jesus' admission that "the Son of Man has come eating and drinking," and the accusation that therefore he was a "glutton and a drunkard" (Mt 11:19), it seems unlikely that Jesus would have been accepted in such circles. He possessed too much of the moderation that characterized main-stream Pharisaism.[2]

There are a number of passages in the Synoptic Gospels which suggest that Jesus may have held extreme views regarding wealth, but on closer examination one finds that this probably was not the case.

And Jesus said, "Foxes have holes, and birds of the air have nests; but the Son of Man has nowhere to lay his head." (Mt 8:20; Lk 9:58)

This could indicate that Jesus was abjectly poor. However, it more likely reflects the typical life of a first-century rabbi who was constantly traveling and thus had no fixed abode.

No servant can serve two masters; for either he will hate one and love the other, or he will be devoted to one and despise the other. You cannot serve God and mammon. (Lk 16:13)

"Love" and "hate" are not always the absolute terms in Hebrew that they are in English. "Love," when contrasted with "hate," can mean "to put first, to prefer."[3] In Luke 14:26 (parallel to Matthew 10:37), for instance, Jesus is quoted as saying that a disciple must "hate" his father, mother, wife, children, brothers, sisters and even himself. Surely Jesus only meant that his disciples must love him above their families and themselves. To "hate" money in any absolute sense is foreign to the general teaching of Jesus and the writers of the New Testament. As Paul said in 1 Timothy 6:10, it is the love of money, not money itself, that is the root of all evil.

He looked up and saw the rich putting their gifts into the treasury; and he saw a poor widow put in two copper coins. And he said, "Amen! I tell you, this poor widow has put in more than all of them; for they all contributed out of their abundance, but she out of her poverty put in all the living that she had." (Lk 21:1-4)

Jesus' statement is probably not an endorsement to give away all one's money. Jesus praised this poor widow because, even though she had given only two small coins, her gift was more sacrificial and proportionately larger than that of the people who had donated much larger sums. Jesus seems to be making the same point as that found in Tobit 4:8-9: "If you have many possessions, make your gift from them in proportion...so you will be laying up a good treasure for yourself against the day of necessity."

"Carry no purse, no bag, no sandals..." (Lk 10:4) — The impression created here is that Jesus instructed his disciples to live in poverty. This is strengthened by Peter's reply in Acts 3:6 to a beggar who asked for alms: "I do not have silver and gold...."[4] One must realize, however, that the disciples did have sandals, bags and purses — they simply were told not to take them on this particular journey. Jesus intended his disciples to be supported during this preaching journey by the families that hosted them.[5]

In addition to being supported during their travels by hospitable families, Jesus and his itinerating band of disciples were also supported by some of the women who accompanied them, such as the wife of one of Herod Antipas' officials. According to Luke 8:3, these women "served them by their wealth." Obviously, Jesus had not required these women to distribute all their wealth to the poor, otherwise they would have had nothing to share with Jesus and his disciples.

Apparently, therefore, Jesus viewed money as a means for good and not only a hindrance to piety. Merely being wealthy did not prevent one's spiritual growth; it was the pursuit of wealth as one's primary goal in life that prevented entrance into the Kingdom of Heaven. One senses a similar attitude behind the praise in the Talmud for the fabulously wealthy Nakdimon (Nicodemus) ben Gurion who, while remaining wealthy, was also very generous in his giving.[6]

> Do not store up for yourselves treasures on earth, where moth and rust devour, and where thieves break in and steal. But store up for yourselves treasures in heaven.... (Mt 6:19–20)

Although this appears to be an instruction to flee from wealth and would seem to indicate that Jesus felt money was inherently evil, it actually is nothing more than Jesus' typical exhortation to prefer the things above, to love the Kingdom of Heaven more than family, wealth, and anything else. In Jesus' view, wealth and the Kingdom of Heaven were not necessarily mutually exclusive, as can be seen from his comments in Matthew 6:33: "Seek first the Kingdom of Heaven and his righteousness and all these things will be yours as well."

Jesus did not condemn a man who happened to be rich. The attitude he expressed was identical to that of a rabbinic source: "If you have been favored with mammon, use it for alms as long as you have it. Obtain [literally, "buy"] with your mammon this world and world to come."[7] It is precisely this idea that lies behind Jesus' exhortation in Luke 16:9 to "make friends for yourselves with the mammon of unrighteousness so that when it fails, you will be received into the eternal habitations."

The Choking Tentacles of Riches

> And as for what fell among the thorns, they are those who hear, but as they go on their way they are choked by the cares and riches and pleasures of life, and their fruit does not mature. (Mt 13:22; Mk 4:18–19; Lk 8:14)

Although Jesus taught that riches might choke the spiritual growth of some disciples, he listed riches as only one of the choking "thorns," and it is doubtful that he meant to give the impression that spiritual unfruitfulness was the necessary result of riches in every case. A man's wealth need not be a spiritual hindrance to him if he uses it to help the poor.

How difficult it is for those who have possessions to come into the Kingdom of God! It is easier for a camel to enter the eye of a needle than for a rich man to come into the Kingdom of God. (Mt 19:23-24; Mk 10:23-25; Lk 18:24-25)

On the surface, Jesus appears to be saying that it is impossible for anyone who is wealthy to receive eternal life. Actually, this metaphor of the camel and the needle's eye is only another of the verbal caricatures that Jesus loved to use. Jesus is saying here no more than what he said in Luke 16:13: One cannot love, that is, put first, two masters. A disciple must choose what is more important to him — mammon or God. As long as a disciple's wealth is not more important than God, as long as it does not prevent him from serving God, then a disciple is free to have possessions.

You lack one thing more. Sell everything you have and give the money to the poor, and you will have treasure in heaven. Then come, follow me. (Mt 19:21; Mk 10:21; Lk 18:22)

This is the only recorded occasion on which Jesus made such a demand, and it seems likely that it was tailored specifically to the condition of the man's heart. Jesus knew that this rich man's money was the most important thing in his life, and because the man loved his possessions more than studying Torah at Jesus' feet, the test of discipleship for him was to give up his wealth. It was not a universal test, and Jesus did not make such a demand of others, even of other rich men. Another prospective disciple might have been asked to give up profession or position in life to prove that he had in fact put the Kingdom of Heaven first.[8]

---

[1] The Hasidim were perhaps the most influential proponents of this philosophy in first-century Israel. These were a stream of Galilean sages who were close in theology to the Pharisees while at the same time in tension with them because the Hasidim emphasized the doing of good deeds more than the study of Torah. Shmuel Safrai carried out extensive research on the Hasidim. He contended that Jesus, though not a Hasid, was similar to the Hasidim in many ways. Safrai argued that Jesus, like the Hasidim, idealized poverty: Jesus lived a pauper's

life, and also demanded of his disciples that they give up all their material wealth. See Shmuel Safrai, "Jesus and the Hasidim," *Jerusalem Perspective* 42, 43 & 44 (Jan–Jun 1994), pp. 3–22. Many outstanding scholars have held Safrai's view regarding Jesus' attitude toward wealth. In his commentary on the Synoptic Gospels, Claude Montefiore quotes Kirsopp Lake (apparently in agreement with Lake): "Professor Lake has said: 'I think Jesus clearly taught that riches ought to be rejected and given to the poor. He not only said so quite definitely to the rich man who asked his advice, but he denied the possibility (apart from the special act of God) that rich men can enter the Kingdom of Heaven. I have not the smallest doubt but that Jesus said this and meant it. I do not believe that he meant it as exceptional teaching. Poverty was his rule of life, yet I do not think it is the right rule of life, or that it is practicable if civilization is to continue' (*The Religion of Yesterday and Tomorrow* [1925], p. 155)" (C. G. Montefiore, *The Synoptic Gospels*, 2nd ed.[London: Macmillan & Co., 1927], 2:559–560).

Vincent Taylor comments on Mark 10:21: "Commentators are right in saying that Jesus does not demand the universal renunciation of property, but gives a command relative to a particular case. Nevertheless, as Lohmeyer, 211, points out, Jesus himself appears to have chosen a life of poverty; He wanders to and fro without a settled home (Mk. i. 39, Lk. ix. 58), His disciples are hungry (Mk. ii. 23, viii. 14), women provide for His needs (Lk. viii. 3), and His disciples can say, '*Idou hemeis aphekamen kai ekolouthekamen soi*' [Behold we left everything and followed you] (Mk. x. 28)" (*The Gospel According to St. Mark* [London: Macmillan & Co., 1952], p. 429). Here, Taylor first seems to agree that Jesus did not idealize poverty, then qualifies his view by quoting another scholar.

Shmuel Safrai has noted: "*Hasidut* [the belief and practice of the Hasidim] is generally associated with the conception of humility" ("Teaching of Pietists in Mishnaic Literature," *The Journal of Jewish Studies* 16 [1956], p. 17, note 13), and it seems likely that in a number of rabbinic passages the word *aniyut* refers not to poverty but to humility.

[2] For an excellent survey of the Pharisaic view that, in general, poverty is an evil, see Israel Abrahams' chapter, "Poverty and Wealth," in *Studies in Pharisaism and the Gospels*, 2 vols. (Cambridge: Cambridge University Press, 1917, 1924; repr. in one volume by Ktav Publishing House, New York, 1967), 1:113–17.

[3] For examples of this Hebraic nuance of "hate," see p. 18.

[4] Also supportive of Safrai's view is the fact that in Acts 2:44–45 we read that the early believers sold their properties and possessions and held all things in common. Compare the story of Ananias and Sapphira (Acts 5:1–11) and Acts 4:34–35. However, note that Peter told Ananias and Sapphira, "While you owned the property, was it not yours to do with as you pleased?" In other words, their only sin was in pretending to have

donated the full amount of the property.

[5] Compare Lk 10:7. See also p. 12.

[6] B. Ketubot 66b-67a. Nakdimon was one of the three wealthiest men in Jerusalem at the beginning of the Roman siege of Jerusalem in A.D. 66. (b. Gittin 56a). The Talmud likewise showers praise upon the convert King Monobaz of Adiabene (mid-first century A.D.) for his generosity in helping those in need. When criticized for dissipating the kingdom's treasures accumulated by his ancestors, Monobas replied: "My ancestors stored up below, but I am storing up above...my ancestors gathered for this world, but I have gathered for the world to come" (b. Bava Batra 11a; *cf.* m. Yoma 3:10; t. Yoma 2:3; Genesis Rabbah 46:10; Josephus, Antiq. 20:75, 92–96).

[7] Derech Eretz Zuta 3:3.

[8] The Kingdom of Heaven is a collective term used by Jesus to refer to his apprenticed disciples. One probably should not draw conclusions about what Jesus advocated for normal life from what he demanded of those select few whom he called to a rigorous life of in-service training. Would Jesus, for instance, have made it a general rule that acceptance of his teaching precluded burying one's father or mother? Stern demands such as those Jesus made of the rich man (Lk 18:22) were directed towards potential disciples, not the general public. It should also be noted that discipleship was not usually permanent. Although a disciple's internship sometimes lasted for years, it was essentially temporary, a period of life devoted to intensive study of Torah.

"Jesus' Attitude Toward Poverty" was adapted and abridged from the article, "Jesus' Attitude To Poverty," by David Bivin, which is available at www.JerusalemPerspective.com.

17.

On Divorce and Remarriage

In the whole of Luke's Gospel, there is just one context in which the verbs "divorce" and "marry" appear together. That passage — only one verse — ought to contribute to a correct understanding of Jesus' attitude toward divorce and remarriage; however, there exists no scholarly consensus on the passage's meaning.

> Any man who divorces his wife and marries another commits adultery, and a man who marries a woman divorced from her husband commits adultery. (Lk 16:18)

In the first half of Luke 16:18, Jesus appears to teach that a man who has divorced his wife should not remarry.[1] In the verse's second half, Jesus seems to say that no man should marry a divorced woman. Does this simplistic interpretation of a difficult verse do justice to Jesus' approach to Torah?

Luke 16:18 is very "Semitic," that is, it is full of Semitic idioms, an indication that Jesus uttered it in Hebrew or Aramaic. A very effective way to approach the verse, then, is to first put its Greek text into Hebrew, and then study the resultant Hebrew text in light of first-century Jewish thought.[2]

Nuances of "And" in Hebrew

The meaning of the Hebrew word usually translated "and" is broad, and its flexibility may be key to understanding this passage. While the English word "and" can mean "also," "as well as," or can be used like a comma to connect words, phrases and sentences, the Hebrew *vav*, (and) can do the work of "but," "or," "so," "then," "because," "therefore," "namely," "since," "while," "on the contrary," and more. Hebrew frequently uses *vav* where English would use no word at all, and in such cases the best translation is simply to drop the "and" entirely. In many instances, to translate *vav* as "and" would obscure the *vav*'s true meaning.[3]

Another meaning of *vav* (and) is "in order to, in order that, so that." Scholars refer to this *vav* as the "*and* of purpose or intention."[4] It occurs frequently in biblical Hebrew, for example: "Let my people go, *and* [i.e., so that] they may worship me in the wilderness" (Ex 7:16).[5] *Vav* (and) in the sense of "in order to" is also attested in Mishnaic or Middle Hebrew, the Hebrew that many scholars believe Jesus spoke.[6]

An example of this usage may exist in Luke 16:18a: "Anyone who divorces his wife *and* marries another commits adultery."[7] The meaning "in order to" fits Luke 16:18a better than simple "and." The Greek text[8] reverts easily and smoothly to beautiful Hebrew: *kol hamegaresh et ishto venose aheret mena'ef* (Anyone who divorces his wife and marries [i.e., in order to marry] another [f.] is committing adultery).[9]

The Debate on Divorce in Jesus' Time

The background to Jesus' saying seems to be a debate between the schools of Shammai and Hillel concerning the grounds for divorce. The debate revolves around the interpretation of an expression found in Deuteronomy 24:1: "After a man has taken a wife and consummated the marriage, if she ceases to please him because he has found an 'indecency of thing' in her, then he shall write her a bill of divorce, hand it to her and send her away from his house."

The expression *ervat davar,* literally, "indecency of thing," is obscure. Consequently, it lends itself to various interpretations, as the rabbinic debate shows:

> The school of Shammai says: "A man may not divorce his wife unless he has found a thing of indecency in her, for it is written, 'because he has found an indecency of thing in her.'" But the school of Hillel says: "[He may divorce her] even if she ruined a dish of food [she prepared for him], for it is written, 'because he has found an indecency of thing in her.'" Rabbi Akiva says: "Even if he found another more beautiful than she, for it is written, 'if she ceases to please him.'"[10]

According to Shammai's interpretation, the emphasis should be on the word "indecency" in the phrase "indecency of thing." Therefore, reversing the order of the words, he interprets the phrase as "a thing of indecency," that is, "something indecent." In his view, marital infidelity is the only grounds for divorce. According to Hillel, however, the emphasis should be on the word, "thing." In Hillel's view, a husband may divorce his wife for anything, for instance, for any imperfection or for any act that is offensive to him. He is permitted to divorce her even for burning his toast. Rabbi Akiva agreed that it is the husband's right to divorce his wife for any cause, illustrating his point with an extreme example: A husband may divorce his wife even if he finds another woman who is more pleasing to him.

A key link to Jesus' saying is the word "another" in Akiva's statement: "Even if he found *aheret*, (another [f.]) more beautiful than she." Jesus' use of this word in a divorce context makes it likely that he was attacking the view espoused by Rabbi Akiva. (Although Akiva lived approximately one hundred years after Jesus, Luke 16:18a suggests that Akiva's view existed in Jesus' day.) Here, Jesus gives a legal opinion. Siding with Shammai, he rules that there is only one cause for divorce — marital unfaithfulness.[11]

If we assume this saying about divorce had two parts, there is a strong possibility that the second part was the second component of a Hebrew doublet. Though superfluous to the Greek ear, repetition of words, phrases, sentences, and even stories, is characteristic of Hebrew. When teaching, Jesus frequently employed doublets (e.g., "tax collectors and sinners" [Mt 11:19, Lk 7:34]) and parallelisms (e.g., "Do not travel Gentile roads, and do not enter Samaritan cities" [Mt 10:5]).[12] If we translate Luke 16:18b to Hebrew, staying as close to the Greek text as the Hebrew language will allow, we get: *vehanose et ha'ishah hamegoreshet mena'ef* (and he who marries the divorced woman commits adultery). An idiomatic translation would yield: "Furthermore, he who marries that divorced woman is committing adultery."[13]

Based on Luke 16:18, we can suppose that Jesus, like Shammai, held that adultery is the only grounds for divorce; and therefore, that Jesus viewed the bill of divorce given by a husband who intends to marry another woman as being invalid from the outset.

Thus, subsequent marriages contracted by the husband or wife are null and void, and any children produced by such marriages are illegitimate. Since future marriages of such a wife have no validity, anyone who marries her will be entering into an adulterous relationship. Should the divorced wife and her second husband learn of the first husband's real motive for divorcing her, they would be obligated to separate immediately.

The second part of Jesus' saying is not addressed to the man who might marry a wife sinfully divorced — the man would not contract the marriage if he were aware of the true reason for the divorce; rather, it is a strengthening of the warning given in the doublet's first part. "Realize the far-reaching consequences of your sinful act," Jesus warns the husband contemplating divorce. "Not only will you yourself commit adultery, you will cause your wife and her second husband to live in adultery." Through marriage, a man and his wife become one flesh (Mt 19:4-6). Should they divorce for reasons other than marital infidelity, any subsequent relationship into which they entered would be adulterous.

Jesus' Innovation

Both parts of Luke 16:18 are exegetical innovations, that is, they are new interpretations of Scripture. The rabbis believed that the Torah was a bottomless well: one could dig deeper and deeper, ever gaining new insights inherent in the Torah given to Moses at Sinai. Jesus spoke of this when he said: "Every scribe trained for the Kingdom of Heaven is like a landlord who brings out of his storeroom new treasures [i.e., innovative interpretations of his own] as well as old [i.e., what he has learned from his teachers]" (Mt 13:52).

The first part of Luke 16:18 is an innovation: Jesus rules that divorcing one's wife in order to marry another is adultery. This statement goes beyond the formulations that Jesus had heard from his teachers. His interpretation "establishes or strengthens" the Torah (Mt 5:17), that is, his innovation reinforces and clarifies the Torah. The second part of the verse is also an innovation, and more startling than the first: the husband who divorces his wife to marry another will not only himself break the seventh of the Ten Commandments, he may cause others to break it.[14]

Grounds for Divorce

Viewed from a Hebraic and Jewish perspective, Luke 16:18 does not address the question of whether divorce is ever permissible. Surely Jesus believed that a husband is permitted to divorce his wife if she is engaged in an adulterous relationship.[15] Nor does Luke 16:18 deal with the permissibility of remarriage after divorce. Jesus probably believed, as did his contemporaries, that both marriage partners, having terminated a marriage with a legally binding bill of divorce, were permitted to remarry.

The church in Corinth wrote to Paul asking for his rulings on several issues relating to marriage. One of these issues was what a follower of Jesus should do about an unbelieving mate whom he or she had married before becoming a believer.[16] Paul's response: "If the unbelieving marriage partner is determined to separate, let him or her do so. The believing man or woman is not bound in such cases. God has called us to live lives of peace" (1 Cor 7:15). In other words, if the unbelieving spouse cannot live with his or her marriage partner's new beliefs, the believing spouse should not attempt, by legal or other means, to prevent the unbelieving partner from separating. By "not bound," Paul also means, presumably, that the believing partner is free to remarry.

In Luke's arrangement, there is no context for Luke 16:18, which is the last in a series of three contextless sayings. In Matthew's Gospel, each of these sayings has its own context, perhaps indicating that Luke or the author of one of Luke's sources has joined these sayings after separating them from their contexts. Does the story in Matthew 19:3–9 (parallel to Mk 10:2–12) provide the original context for Luke 16:18? Though conjectural, I suggest the following reconstruction:

> And Pharisees approached him and tested him, saying, "May a man divorce his wife for any reason?" He answered and said, "Have you not read that he who created them, from the beginning made them male and female, and said, 'Thus it is that a man leaves his father and mother and cleaves to his wife, and the two become one flesh'? So they are no longer two but one flesh. What therefore God has joined, let no one separate." They said to him, "Why then

did Moses command to give a certificate of divorce and to divorce?" He said to them, "Because of your hardness of heart Moses permitted you to divorce your wives, but from the beginning it was not so. But I say to you, anyone who divorces his wife to marry another woman is committing adultery; furthermore, he who marries that divorced woman is committing adultery."

What Would Jesus Do?

What would Jesus have said to a man who had divorced, or was about to divorce, his wife in order to marry another? We can suppose that, since he abhorred divorce,[17] he would have spoken sternly to the man. He would have told him (paraphrasing Luke 16:18): "It is detestable for you to divorce the 'wife of your youth,' the one who has shared your life and stood by you for years, in order to marry a younger, more physically attractive woman. In addition, your sin may cause others to enter adulterous relationships."

However, Jesus would have tempered his stern rebuke with compassion. He would have tried to restore the marriage. If neither the man nor his wife had yet contracted another marriage, he would have urged the man to repent and be reconciled to his wife. If the man showed a readiness to repent, before concluding the conversation, Jesus probably would have said to the man, as he did to the woman caught in adultery, "Go and sin no more."

This study illustrates how important rabbinic literature can be for gaining a perspective that allows accurate interpretation of gospel texts. The study also shows that the Synoptic Gospels' Hebraic background can often provide the necessary clues for understanding Jesus' words. Furthermore, the study demonstrates that even the most insignificant grammatical feature of Hebrew — in this case, one nuance of a one-letter word — can be important for understanding the teaching of Jesus.

The "and" in Luke 16:18a is probably the Semitic "and of purpose." This idiom together with, in the same context, the word "another" strengthen the likelihood that the background to Jesus' statement was a rabbinic debate on the meaning of *ervat davar* (indecency of thing) in Deuteronomy 24:1. Like Shammai, Jesus interpreted the expression as "a thing of indecency," that is, marital infidelity, strongly opposing Hillel's interpretation, which allowed a man to divorce his wife "for any cause."

Many a faithful Christian woman has been discarded by a husband who has found "another more beautiful than she." Though innocent, she has suffered humiliation and public ostracism. Because of her understanding of Scripture, she may have remained single the rest of her life, considering it a sin to remarry. Jesus' words should act as a warning: a husband who divorces his wife "to marry another" sets in motion a chain of disasters — in his life and the lives of many others.

---

[1] Thus, apparently, Jesus would not consider a man an adulterer if he divorced his wife but did not remarry.

[2] For a discussion of Semitic Greek of the Synoptic Gospels and its use in investigating the wording of Jesus' sayings, see pp. xxiii–xxvi.

[3] The Greek word *kai* (the equivalent of *vav*) can mean "and," "also," "even," "just," "as," and in certain expressions, "or." See Henry George Liddell and Robert Scott, *A Greek-English Lexicon*, revised and augmented by Henry Stuart Jones with Roderick McKenzie (Oxford: Clarendon Press, 1968), pp. 857–858. Grammars and lexicons of New Testament Greek can be misleading since, often, the only support they provide for a particular nuance of *kai* is a citation from the Synoptic Gospels. Such citations may merely reflect the Synoptic Gospels' Semitic background.

[4] See Francis Brown, with the cooperation of S. R. Driver and Charles Briggs, *The New Brown-Driver-Briggs-Gesenius Hebrew and English Lexicon* (Peabody, MA: Hendrickson Publishers, 1979; reprint of *Hebrew and English Lexicon of the Old Testament* [London: Oxford University Press, 1907]), p. 254. The best categorization of the nuances of *vav* (with biblical examples of each) is found in *A New Concordance of the Bible*, ed. Abraham Even-Shoshan (Jerusalem: Kiryath Sepher, 1987), p. 317 (Hebrew).

[5] Other examples are: "I will not accept so much as a thread or the thong of a sandal belonging to you, *and* [i.e., so that] you will not be able to say, 'It is I who made Abram rich'" (Gen 14:23); "Do this *and* [i.e., so that] you may live" (Gen 42:18); "They [Aaron and his sons] shall wash in water *and* [i.e., so that] they will not die" (Ex 30:21).

[6] For example: "He who begins to wish that his wife will die and [i.e., in order that] he will inherit her property, or that she will die and [i.e., in

order that] he will marry her sister..." (t. Sotah 5:10).

⁷ John Nolland has suggested that the subject of Mark 10:11–12 and parallels is divorce for the sake of remarriage ("The Gospel Prohibition of Divorce: Tradition History and Meaning," *Journal for the Study of the New Testament* 58 [1995], p. 33). Nolland asserts that the Greek church fathers often understood *kai* (and) in the phrase "and marries another" (Mt 19:9; Mk 10:11; Lk 16:18) as denoting purpose; however, he gives no examples of this usage.

There is also one New Testament version whose translator recognized this idiom: *The New Testament: A Private Translation in the Language of the People* by Charles B. Williams (Chicago: Moody Press, 1958). Williams' translation of Luke 16:18a reads: "Any man who divorces his wife to marry another woman commits adultery." Williams added a footnote to the word "to" of his translation: "*And*, in Aramaic source, expressing purpose." As to Williams' reference to Aramaic, it must be pointed out that the idiom also exists in Hebrew.

⁸ Including the opening Greek words, *pas ho* (meaning, "anyone or everyone who..."), the equivalent of the Hebrew words *kol ha-* or *kol she-* (anyone or everyone who...), that are so typical of rabbinic sayings. Compare, for example, these sayings from the Mishnah: "Anyone who honors the Torah is himself honored by others" (m. Avot 4:6); and "Anyone who fulfills the Torah in poverty will in the end fulfill it in wealth" (m. Avot 4:9).

The *pas ho* construction is as frequent in the Gospels as in rabbinic literature. For example: Matthew 5:22 ("anyone who is angry with his brother"); Matthew 5:28 ("anyone who looks at a woman lustfully"); Matthew 7:26 ("everyone who hears these words of mine"); Luke 14:11 ("everyone who exalts himself will be humbled"); and Luke 20:18 ("everyone who falls on that stone").

⁹ For examples of the expression *hamegaresh et ishto...* (the [man] who divorces his wife...), see m. Gittin 8:9 and 9:1.

¹⁰ M. Gittin 9:10.

¹¹ In several instances Jesus' rulings follow those of Shammai rather than Hillel. Where the status of women is at issue, Jesus' rulings, like Shammai's, always strengthen the woman's position. See J. N. Epstein's discussion of Mark 7:11–12 (= Mt 15:5) and Matthew 23:16–18 in his *Introduction to Tannaitic Literature: Mishna, Tosephta and Halakhic Midrashim* (Jerusalem: Magnes Press, and Tel Aviv: Dvir, 1957), pp. 377–78 (Hebrew).

It is frequently assumed that Jesus was closer in outlook to Hillel than to Shammai. That is not true, as Jesus' teaching on divorce shows. According to Shmuel Safrai, Jews in the Galilee usually followed the *halachot* of Shammai (private communication), which often were stricter than those of Hillel. Since Jesus was a Galilean, we should not be surprised that he gave rulings which agree with the opinions of

Shammai.

[12] Parallelism — expressing the same thought in two or more different, though synonymic, ways — is the hallmark of Hebrew poetry. Other examples of Hebrew-style doublets in the Synoptic Gospels are: "eating and drinking...a glutton and a drunkard" (Mt 11:19; Lk 7:34); "the wise and understanding" (Lk 10:21); "prophets and apostles" (Lk 11:49); and "kings and governors" (Lk 21:12).

[13] There is another possible interpretation of Luke 16:18b, assuming Luke 16:18 was originally a Hebraic doublet. Jesus may have said: "Any man who divorces his wife and marries another is committing adultery, and any woman who divorces her husband and marries another is committing adultery." According to Jewish halachah, a woman cannot divorce her husband; the husband alone can declare a divorce. However, she can scheme to end a marriage relationship in order to marry another.

Brad H. Young suggests a third interpretation of Luke 16:18b (Jesus the Jewish Theologian [Peabody, MA: Hendrickson, 1995], pp. 114–15). Young notes that in Jewish halachah a woman who is divorced because of an adulterous relationship is not permitted to marry her paramour (m. Sotah 5:1); therefore, Luke 16:18b ("he who marries a woman divorced from her husband commits adultery") could mean, "he who marries a woman who obtained a divorce merely for the sake of her second marriage commits adultery." In this interpretation, however, Jesus' statement would not be an exegetical innovation.

[14] Shmuel Safrai points out that an innovation, or its most powerful formulation, usually comes at the end of a sage's teaching. He believes that Shammai would have been very impressed had he heard Jesus' statement, and would have remarked: "Yes, that's right! That is the logical extension of my ruling that a man may not divorce his wife unless he has found 'a thing of indecency' in her" (private communication).

[15] Scripture records that even God himself issued a bill of divorce on the grounds of adultery (Jer 3:8; Is 50:1).

[16] Although not stated explicitly in 1 Corinthians 7:15, we may assume that Paul is relating to members of the community who married before becoming believers. This assumption is supported by other statements of the apostle, such as his rule that if a woman's husband dies, she is permitted to remarry, "but he [her second husband] must belong to the Lord" (1 Cor 7:39). Paul forbade the Corinthians to "be unequally yoked with unbelievers" (2 Cor 6:14), perhaps referring to marriage with an unbeliever. Thus, The New English Bible translates: "Do not unite yourselves with unbelievers; they are no fit mates for you."

[17] Notice that God detests a husband who divorces "the wife of your marriage covenant":

You also do this: You cover the LORD's altar with tears. You weep and moan because he no longer pays attention to your oblations or accepts what you offer. You ask, "Why?" It is because the LORD is a witness between you and the wife of your youth, whom you have betrayed, though she is your partner, the wife of your marriage covenant.... Do not betray the wife of your youth. "I detest divorce," says the LORD, the God of Israel.... (Mal 2:13–16)

Compare the warnings in Proverbs 5:1–23 and 6:20–7:27 to flee the adulteress. Notice especially the reference to "the wife of your youth" in 5:18. Also, see Isaiah 54:6, "Like a wife deserted and dejected, like a wife of youth who has been rejected."

"On Divorce and Remarriage" was adapted and abridged from the article, "'And' or 'In order to' Remarry," by David Bivin, available at www.JerusalemPerspective.com.

IV.
The Kingdom
Is Here

18.

Seeing and Hearing
the Kingdom of Heaven

But blessed are your eyes, for they see, and your ears, for
they hear. Truly, I say to you, many prophets and
righteous men longed to see what you see, and did not
see it, and to hear what you hear, and did not hear it. (Mt
13:16–17, RSV)

Before we discuss the meaning of Jesus' statement, let us
search for its context. Where do these verses belong in the
chronology of events in Jesus' life? It is probable that, as the Gospel
of Luke records, the original context of Jesus' saying was the return
of Jesus' disciples from their great healing and preaching mission
(Lk 10:1–12).[1] The disciples were excited: "Lord, even the demons
are subject to us in your name!" (vs. 17). Jesus was excited, too: "I
was watching Satan fall like lightening from heaven!" (vs. 18). And
Jesus gave thanks that his heavenly father had concealed "these
things" (probably, *razei el*, the secret things, or mysteries, of God)
from the "wise and understanding" (the self-righteous?), but had
revealed them to his disciples (vs. 21). It was at this point that Jesus
uttered the "Blessed are your eyes that see and your ears that hear"
saying. Perhaps the continuation was another saying that preserved
the "seeing and hearing" idiom: "To you it has been given to know
the mysteries of God [*razei el*], but for others they are in parables
so that seeing they may not see, and hearing they may not hear"
(Lk 8:10).

Seeing the Kingdom of Heaven

If the context of these words of Jesus is the Lukan context, then
Jesus, as in so many other passages, was teaching about the

Kingdom of Heaven. One would not imagine that a spiritual realm such as the Kingdom of Heaven could be perceived by an organ of sense, yet apparently Jesus made a connection between it and the sense of sight.[2] This same connection may be found in rabbinic sources. A number of passages spring to mind.

In the Sabbath evening synagogue prayers, we find these beautiful words, literally, "Your Kingdom saw your sons splitting the sea before Moses," that is, "Your sons [the Israelites] witnessed the Kingdom of Heaven when you [God] split the Red Sea so that Moses and the Israelites could pass." Here we notice the connection between the verb "see" and God's Kingdom. This saying, like Jesus' "If it is by the finger of God that I cast out demons, then the Kingdom of God has come upon you" (Lk 11:20), demonstrates that in first-century Jewish thinking, when one witnessed a miracle of God, one saw his Kingdom.

In an ancient rabbinical commentary on the Book of Exodus an amazing statement by Rabbi Eliezer is recorded:

> How does one know that at the [Red] Sea even the maidservants saw what Isaiah and Ezekiel never were fortunate enough to see? Because Scripture says about them, "And through the prophets I gave parables." [Hos 12:10][3]

In other words, God did not reveal himself even to the prophets in the same mighty way that he did to the whole people, great and small, at the Red Sea. What did these humble servant girls see? They witnessed a great demonstration of God's power, the dividing of the Red Sea. They saw God's Kingdom.

Hearing the Kingdom of Heaven

Since in Matthew 13:16-17 "hear" is used by Jesus as the parallel to "see," it is natural to expect additional examples of "hear" plus "Kingdom of Heaven" in the teaching of Jesus and his contemporaries.[4]

How can one hear the Kingdom of Heaven? To better understand what Jesus probably meant when he spoke of seeing and hearing, we should examine the story of Jesus and the messengers sent by John the Baptist (Mt 11:2-6; Lk 7:18-19, 22-23).

Apparently, in John's eyes, Jesus was not accomplishing the messianic task. Consequently, John began to have second thoughts about his identification of Jesus as the one who would "baptize you with the Holy Spirit and fire" (Mt 3:11). Jesus was not burning the chaff with "unquenchable fire" (that is, "destroying sinners") as John had prophesied; rather, Jesus was engaged in restorative works.

In rabbinic fashion, John's disciples asked Jesus: "Are you the 'Coming One' [Zech 9:9; Mal 3:1]?" To which Jesus responded: "Report to John what you have seen and heard" (Lk 7:22). What had John's disciples seen during their stay with Jesus? Miracles! The sick and disabled restored to health, even the dead raised to life. What had they heard? The preaching of good news to the spiritually hungry and humble. Thus, "hearing," as well as "seeing," was appropriate to "Kingdom of Heaven."

We receive further confirmation from the account of the Sending of the Twelve Disciples (Lk 9:1-6; 10:1-12; Mt 10:1-16). As a result of their pivotal mission, these twelve were later to be known as apostles (sent ones, emissaries). As they extended the ministry of Jesus, their work, too, was characterized by "seeing and hearing." In every town they entered, they first healed the sick and then declared: "The Kingdom of Heaven has come near you [that is, has arrived]!" Each miracle occurred through God's supernatural intervention and Jesus' disciples simply attested that God was reigning at that moment, in that place, over that situation. The people Jesus' disciples encountered "saw" and "heard" the Kingdom of Heaven. What did these people see? Just what John's two disciples had seen — miracles. And what did they hear? Just what John's disciples had heard — the good news that the Kingdom of Heaven had come.

Summation

Matthew 13:16-17 doesn't sound to an English reader like anything of great importance — just something about eyes and ears and prophets and righteous men. Without a knowledge of the saying's context, and without its Jewish and Hebraic background, it is quite prosaic. However, if this saying deals with Jesus' central theme, the Kingdom of Heaven, then it would be one of the most exciting and important verses in the Bible!

Jesus continually taught about the Kingdom of Heaven, his work of restoration and salvation. He was busy seeking and saving the lost sons of Abraham, liberating those that Satan had taken captive by healing their illnesses and casting out their demons. In his teaching Jesus continually implied that he was the king of the Kingdom of Heaven. Because of the rich Scriptural traditions with which contemporary Jewish society was equipped, there was usually no need for Jesus to even mention the term "Kingdom of Heaven." By dropping allusions — for instance, to the monumental miracle of the splitting of the Red Sea — Jesus could communicate with great economy of words that the messianic age for which the prophets had yearned, the Kingdom of Heaven, had arrived.

These few simple words of Jesus' about seeing and hearing have a powerful message. Not only did Jesus hint that the miracles that his disciples had recently witnessed and even, in his name, performed themselves, were the demonstration of the Kingdom of Heaven, but also with these words he made the prodigious claim that he himself was the long-awaited Messiah of Israel. It would be hard to find a more powerful statement in the teachings of Jesus!

---

[1] The author of Luke places Jesus' words about the blessed eyes and ears after Jesus' rejoicing in the Holy Spirit (Lk 10:21–22) and before the *Lawyer's Question* (Lk 10:25–28); however, Matthew's author places them in an entirely different context — following *The Reason for Speaking in Parables* (Mt 13:10–15) [probably because of the common words "see" and "hear" in Mt 13:13–15] and before *The Interpretation of the Parable of the Sower* (Mt 13:18–23). Because Jesus' words were first recorded out of order and context, his sayings are sometimes found in differing settings in different Gospels (see pp. 36–37).

[2] Note Manson's comment: "The blessedness consists not in the fact that their eyes are open (as in Mt.), but in the fact that there is something to be seen by the open-eyed, the manifestation, namely, of the kingdom of God" (T. W. Manson, *The Sayings of Jesus*, [London: SCM, 1974 (1949)], 80).

[3] Mechilta, Beshallah 3; on Exodus 15:2 (ed. Horovitz-Rabin, 126, lines 19–20). This rabbinic parallel to Matthew 13:16–17 has been noted. For example, S. T. Lachs quoted Rabbi Eliezer's statement, calling it "an interesting parallel" to Mt 13:17; but did not elaborate. See Samuel

Tobias Lachs, *A Rabbinic Commentary on the New Testament: The Gospels of Matthew, Mark and Luke* (Hoboken, NJ: Ktav, 1987), p. 221.

4 Shmuel Safrai kindly provided me with this tantalizing rabbinic example: Exodus 20:18 reads, "Now when all the people saw the thunder and lightning, the din of the ram's horn and the mountain smoking, they were afraid and fell back...." The rabbis, noticing the unusual phrase "saw the thunder," discussed how something that normally is perceived with the ear could be perceived with the eye: "'They saw what was visible and heard what was audible' — Rabbi Ishmael. Rabbi Akiva, however, said: 'They saw and heard what was visible, they saw words of fire proceeding out of the mouth of the Power [i.e., God] and being carved upon the tablets, as it is said, "The voice of the LORD carves out [with] flames of fire [Pss 29:7]"'" (Mechilta, Yithro 9; on Exodus 20:15 [ed. Horovitz-Rabin, 235, lines 8–10]).

"Seeing and Hearing the Kingdom of Heaven" was adapted from the article, "Seeing (and Hearing!) the Kingdom of Heaven," by David Bivin, available at www.JerusalemPerspective.com.

19.

"Prophet" as a Messianic Title

Jesus spoke of himself using many messianic titles from Scripture. Names such as "Son of Man" in Luke 19:10, the "Green Tree" in Luke 23:31, and "King" in Matthew 25:34 all have their origins in messianic passages from the Hebrew Scriptures. Others referred to Jesus by such messianic titles as: "Lord" (Lk 5:8), the "Son of God" (Lk 1:35) and "Son of David" (Lk 18:38).

Jesus the Prophet

One title applied to Jesus is not so clearly messianic: "Prophet." There can be little doubt that Jesus viewed himself as a prophet, and that many of his contemporaries concurred. Jesus claimed to be a prophet when he quoted the popular saying, "No one is a prophet in his own village," going on to compare himself to Elijah and Elisha (Lk 4:24-27). He made the same claim when he said, "It cannot be that a prophet should perish away from Jerusalem" (Lk 13:33).

But what did the people of Nain have in mind when they exclaimed, "A great prophet has been raised in our midst!"? Since they had just witnessed the bringing to life of a dead man, a miracle that also had been performed by Elijah (1 Kings 17:17-24) and Elisha (2 Kings 4:18-37), one might conclude that the people viewed Jesus as a prophet of the stature of these or other biblical prophets. However, the language of their exclamation suggests a connection with a scriptural passage that points to a more radical conclusion.

Prophecy of Moses

Moses told the people: "A prophet from your midst, from your brothers, like me, will raise for you the Lord your God. To him you must listen" (a literal translation of Deuteronomy 18:15).

These words, and those used by the inhabitants of Nain, are too similar to be coincidental. Both passages speak of "a prophet" in the singular and without the definite article; the Deuteronomic passage has "will raise" and "from your midst," while the Lukan passage has "has been raised" and "in our midst."

Perhaps Moses' statement in Deuteronomy 18 originally referred to his successor, Joshua. Surprisingly, however, one does not read at the end of the book of Deuteronomy that Joshua was a prophet like Moses, but rather, "Since then no prophet has arisen in Israel like Moses...no one has ever shown the mighty power and performed the awesome deeds that Moses did in the sight of all Israel" (Deut 34:10, 12).

This statement may have indicated to some that the "prophet like Moses" was not Joshua, but someone yet to come. In the post-biblical period, Moses' statement often was interpreted as referring to a messianic figure: the "Second Moses," the "Prophet of the Last Days."

Risto Santala points out an intriguing rabbinic interpretation that supports the idea that the Messiah would be a prophet comparable to Moses:

> Like the first redeemer so is the last redeemer. Just as it is said of the first redeemer, "And Moses took his wife and sons and put them on a donkey" (Ex 4:20), so it is said of the last redeemer, "Gentle and riding on a donkey." [Zech 9:9][1]

This interpretation, attributed to Rabbi Isaac, cannot be dated before the end of the third century A.D., but it may have originated in an earlier period. Notice how the "last redeemer," the humble Messiah who comes riding on a donkey, is compared to the "first redeemer," Moses. It is interesting that Stephen also referred to Moses as *"redeemer"* in his speech to the Sanhedrin (Acts 7:35). Also, the two disciples that met the resurrected Jesus on the Emmaus Road declared Jesus a prophet and then immediately mentioned their hope that he was the one to redeem Israel (Lk 24:19, 21).

Greater than Moses

According to the rabbis, "There is no one in Israel greater than he [i.e., Moses][2] "However, there is a rabbinic tradition that refers to the Messiah as being more exalted than Moses:[3]

> It is written, "Who are you, O great mountain? Before Zerubbabel you will become level ground" [Zech 4:7]. What is "Who are you, O great mountain"? This is the King Messiah. And why is he called "a great mountain"? Because he is greater than the patriarchs...elevated beyond Abraham, exalted above Moses and superior to the ministering angels.[4]

This tradition of exalting the Messiah above Moses may be the reason the Nainites added "great" to their allusion to Moses' prophecy. It is interesting that the angel Gabriel promised Mary that Jesus would be "great" (Lk 1:32).

A Trustworthy Prophet

Since of Moses it was said, "He is trusted throughout my house" (Num 12:7), the "prophet of the last days" came to be regarded, like Moses, as the "trustworthy prophet."

Even a century or more before the time of Jesus there was the expectation among the people that God would send this "trustworthy prophet." In 140 B.C., a great assembly of the people and its leaders resolved that Simon the Maccabee would be "their leader and High Priest forever until a trustworthy prophet will arise" (1 Macc 14:41). This is a reference to the "prophet like Moses" who would one day appear. Likewise, Hebrews 3:1–6 draws a comparison between Moses and Jesus emphasizing the trustworthiness of the two.

Messiah: The Prophet

Some of the strongest evidence for the existence of the early Jewish belief that the Messiah would be "the prophet" promised by Moses comes from the New Testament. For instance, one sees from sermons recorded in the Book of Acts that the earliest disciples preached Jesus as the fulfillment of Deuteronomy 18:15. Both Peter and Stephen quoted this scripture and related it to Jesus (Acts 3:22; 7:37; cf. Jn. 7:40).

A further indication that Jesus was seen as the "Second Moses" of Deuteronomy 18:15 is found in the New Testament in the Transfiguration account. The heavenly voice pronounced Jesus to be "my son, my chosen," and commanded "to him listen" (Lk 9:35). This "to him listen" is the same command found in Deuteronomy 18:15.

From such passages in the New Testament, and from other contemporary Jewish sources, it seems clear that the title "prophet" was often used to mean more than prophet. Those who applied it to Jesus may have used it as a synonym for "Messiah."

---

[1] Ecclesiastes Rabbah 1:9; Risto Santala, *The Messiah in the Old Testament in the Light of Rabbinical Writings* (Jerusalem: Keren Ahvah Meshihit, 1993), p. 59.

[2] *En beyisrael gadol mimenu* (Mechilta, Beshallah; to Exodus 13:19 [ed. Horovitz-Rabin, p. 79, lines 5–6]).

[3] David Flusser, *Jewish Sources in Early Christianity* [New York: Adama Books, 1987], pp. 64–65.

[4] Tanhuma, Toledot 134–138 [ed. Buber, p. 139]; to Isaiah 52:13; compare the parallel in Sifre to Numbers 12:3–7.

"'Prophet' as a Messianic Title" was adapted from the article, "'Prophet' as a Messianic Title," by David Bivin, which is available online at www.JerusalemPerspective.com.

20.

The Strength of Weakness

The Bible uses many synonyms for spiritual weakness. These are words often used in the book of Isaiah and the Beatitudes of Jesus: "poor," "poor in spirit," "lowly in spirit," "broken hearted," "humble," "mourner," "hungry for righteousness." These synonyms indicate that the people of God are those who realize their utter dependence on him. They realize that by themselves they are nothing, they have nothing, and they can do nothing unless God enables them. Only when we admit our inability and weakness can

Jesus healing the crippled man by the pool of Bethesda. (Jn 5:1-8)

we live victoriously. But not only must we be aware of our total weakness, we must see it as a form of blessing.

This important spiritual principle is described in the famous passage about the great heroes of our faith, Hebrews 11. The writer summarizes this principle in just three Greek words: *edynamothesan apo astheneias* — "whose weakness was turned to strength" (Heb 11:34).

Only when we realize our spiritual inability can God operate in us and through us. Only when we look to God rather than relying on our own strength can God use us. Even that is not enough — not only must we recognize our weakness, but we must be content with that situation and give God thanks.

Paul the apostle had learned this principle when he wrote his letter to the Corinthians:

> But he [the LORD] said to me, "My grace is sufficient for you, for in weakness my power is perfected." Therefore I will boast all the more gladly about my weaknesses, so that Christ's power may rest on me. That is why, for Christ's sake, I am pleased with weaknesses, insults, hardships, persecutions, and difficulties. For when I am weak, then I am strong. (2 Cor 12:9–10)

Faith as Dependence on God

Emunah (faith, belief) is closely related to spiritual weakness. Biblical faith is not so much belief in someone or something as persistence. It is "hanging in there" in spite of the circumstances. But faith is also the recognition of our dependence on God.

For me the story which best illustrates Abraham's faith is his response to God's promise that he would have a successor. When the three angels visited his encampment, he was 99 and Sarah was 89 — a young woman! There was not a chance of Sarah becoming pregnant: "Abraham and Sarah were already old and well advanced in years, and Sarah was past the age of childbearing." Abraham knew that God would have to perform a miracle. He knew his own weakness, and that was precisely were his strength lay.

When the Israelites stood before the Red Sea with the Egyptian army behind them, their only hope was the LORD — but that was their strength.

Samson was strong only when he trusted in the LORD. When he began to trust in his own strength, he was defeated. He was humbled and punished with the loss of his sight, but when he finally began again to trust in the LORD, he gained his greatest victory.

At Peniel Jacob was so desperate, so afraid of what his brother would do to him the next day, that he refused to go on without meeting the LORD. In so many words he said, "I can't face tomorrow without you, LORD." This was the beginning of his dependence on God and the beginning of victory for him. I don't completely understand this story, but its significance seems to be that the angel weakened him by crippling him. He went away from that meeting limping, but spiritually he was a new and stronger man.

In the Bible, widows are often used as examples of faith. Consider the parable of the unjust judge and the widow in Luke 18:1–8. In ancient times, a widow's situation often was hopeless; and yet when a widow depended on God, out of her hopelessness came deliverance.

The ultimate example of weakness was Jesus on the cross. He was nailed down, unable to move. No one could help him. Even God did not save his life. Yet out of this ultimate weakness came the ultimate victory: "For to be sure, he was crucified in weakness, yet he lives by God's power. Likewise, we are weak in him, yet by God's power we will live with him to serve you" (2 Cor 13:4).

The Samson syndrome is a great danger for us. When Samson was strong he began to depend on his own strength. This is our natural tendency. The minute God does something for us spiritually, we begin to think we are strong and begin to be independent. The Pharisee thought: "Thank you LORD that I am not as bad as that tax collector." And we think to ourselves, "Thank you LORD that I am not like that Pharisee in Jesus' parable," or "Thank you LORD that I am not as bad as this or that sinner."

We have to believe every moment of our lives, just as in that first moment when we met Jesus, "I cannot make it on my own." The minute we give up and admit our weakness, victory begins.

The confession of our limitations brings great release and spiritual freedom, just as our first confession in coming to Jesus brought a great release. Now we can stop striving and relax. It's the Greyhound bus mentality: "Take a bus and leave the driving to us." We must relax and let God do the driving — let him have full control.

I can do all things through the Messiah who gives me strength, but I can do nothing without him. 1 Corinthians 1:25–27 is a good summary of this:

> For the foolishness of God is wiser than man's wisdom, and the weakness of God is stronger than man's strength. Brothers, think of what you were when you were called. Not many of you were wise by human standards; not many were influential; not many were of noble birth. But God chose the foolish things of the world to shame the wise; God chose the weak things of the world to shame the strong.

"The Strength of Weakness" was adapted from the article, "The Strength of Weakness," by David Bivin, which is available online at www.JerusalemPerspective.com.

21.

Requirements for Gentiles

Christians often have distanced themselves so far from their Jewish roots and heritage that they have forgotten that they, too, are obligated by commandments. On the question of whether there was such an obligation, leaders of the embryonic church ruled that followers of Jesus of non-Jewish parentage were obligated to keep a few, universal commandments. Unlike the Jewish disciples of Jesus, Gentiles were not obligated to be circumcised (although apparently they were asked to undergo proselyte immersion) or to undertake the obligations of the Sinai Covenant.

How many biblical commandments were Gentile followers of Jesus commanded to keep by the leaders of the new community? The obligatory commandments are listed in Acts 15:20.

In the early forties of the first century A.D., the "apostles and elders" (Acts 15:6) of Jesus' community, who included Simon Peter and Jesus' brother James, gathered in Jerusalem to discuss what they should do with the increasing number of non-Jewish followers of Jesus. These leaders were not indecisive. They ruled, contrary to the opinion of "those who were zealous for the Torah," such as James, that Gentiles would be required to observe only a few central commandments.

Agreeing with Peter's recommendation (Acts 15:7–11), the assembly decided to "loose" (that is, absolve) the Gentiles from the obligation of undergoing circumcision and from the observance of the biblical commandments prescribed in the Torah of Moses. However, in accordance with James' recommendation, the assembled leaders decided to "bind" (that is, "prohibit")[1] in the sense of obligating converts to this new sect of Judaism to observe three basic, universal and overriding commandments that within Judaism later developed into seven commandments known as the "Commandments of Noah" or the "Noachide Commandments."

According to Acts 15:19–20, "those of the Gentiles who are turning to God in repentance" were commanded to abstain from:

1. "pollutions of idols"
2. "sexual immorality"
3. "things strangled"
4. "blood"

With slight variations the list of prohibitions is repeated in Acts 15:29 and 21:25.[2] Manuscripts of the Books of Acts are split between a list of three prohibitions (omitting either "strangled" or "immorality") and a list of four. This situation seems to indicate that there was uncertainty among ancient editors and copyists about the original reading.

Because of the uncertainty in the texts, two opinions have formed among scholars regarding the original intent of the list. One scholar suggests that the original prohibitions were ritual – focusing on practices used in idolatrous worship. Others have argued that the original prohibitions were basic moral laws that may have been misunderstood by copyists who didn't recognize the Jewish idioms used in the list of prohibitions.[3]

Evidence from early Jewish and Christian sources seems to support this second conclusion. The three great sins of "idolatry, immorality, and murder," occur frequently in rabbinic sources. This triplet also can be found in early Christian sources.[4] They represent the essentials of the biblical commandments, God's most basic demands of humankind. In Jewish thought of Jesus' time, not only were idolatry, murder and immorality the classic characteristics of Gentiles,[5] but Israel's sages sometimes accused the nation of these same central sins. Failure to keep the three, it was said, resulted in the exile.[6]

The Hebrew terms for these three great prohibitions are: *avodah zarah* (idolatry; literally, "foreign worship"); *gilui arayot* (forbidden marriages [including adultery] and sexual relationships; literally, "uncovering of nakedness"); and *shefichut damim* (murder; literally, "shedding of bloods.") Each of these prohibitions encompasses a number of biblical commands: *avodah zarah* includes the prohibitions found in Exodus 20:4–5; 23:13; Leviticus 19:4; and Deuteronomy 16:21–22; *gilui arayot* includes the sexual relationships enumerated in Leviticus 18:6–18; *shefichut damim* includes the prohibitions recorded in Exodus 20:13; Leviticus 19:16; Numbers 35:12, 28, 31, 32; and Deuteronomy 5:17; 19:2; 21:4.

The term, *shefichut damim* (shedding of bloods), containing an idiomatic reference to "bloods," could have caused "blood" to enter the list of prohibitions. Later Greek editors and copyists may have wrongly assumed that the text referred to the biblical prohibition against eating meat from which the blood had not been properly drained. In turn, the reference to "blood" may have drawn "things strangled" into the list, essentially, the same prohibition against eating the meat of animals that had not been correctly slaughtered, in this case, an animal that had been put to death by strangulation rather than by the slitting of the throat. Once "blood" and "things strangled" were attached to the list, then "(the pollutions of) idolatry" was misunderstood to mean "[meat] sacrificed to idols." In this fashion, three central moral prohibitions became misunderstood as food laws.

If this hypothesis is true, then the universal commandments that the leaders of the early church required of its Gentile converts were the same commandments that the nation as a whole expected righteous Gentiles, or God-fearers, to keep. This explains why James (and the other zealous members of the early church) suggested that these minimal commands be "bound" upon Gentiles who came to faith in Jesus. The Jerusalem council did not innovate, but rather ruled in accordance with usual Jewish expectations of Gentiles.

Apparently, the Apostolic Council's ruling was that non-Jewish converts were required to observe only three commandments: abstinence from idolatry, sexual immorality and murder — in Jewish eyes, the absolute minimal observance of the Torah. Since Jews expected righteous Gentiles to observe these prohibitions, it was only natural that the first community of Jesus, a new Jewish sect, should have prohibited these sins to converts of non-Jewish origin. James, and others like him, must have reasoned: since these converts were born in a grossly sinful, pagan environment, they should not be obligated to keep the numerous commandments of the Written and Oral Torah. Such observance would be more than could be reasonably expected. If the Gentiles would stop worshiping false gods, committing murder and engaging in sexual immorality, that would be sufficient!

---

[1] For more on the rabbinic idea of binding and loosing, see pp. 98–99.

[2] "To abstain from idol sacrifices, and blood, and things strangled and sexual immorality" (Acts 15:29); "To keep themselves from idol sacrifice, and blood, and a thing strangled and sexual immorality" (Acts 21:25).

[3] For a discussion of the textual variants found in the manuscripts of these three lists (Acts 15:20, 29: 21:25), and the commentators who have argued for four, three (and even two) original prohibitions, see Bruce M. Metzger, *A Textual Commentary on the Greek New Testament* (London: United Bible Societies, 1975), pp. 429–34.

Metzger suggests that the original prohibitions — ritual, not moral — are the four found in the Alexandrian textual tradition: "against eating food offered to idols, things strangled and blood, and against *porneia* (however this latter is to be interpreted)." He argues that this fourfold ritual decree, or food law, was later altered in the Western textual tradition into a threefold moral law, "to refrain from idolatry, unchasity and blood-shedding (or murder), to which is added the negative [form] of the Golden Rule" by dropping the reference to "strangled" and by adding the negative Golden Rule (pp. 431–32).

However, David Flusser ("The Jewish-Christian Schism, Part I," *Immanuel* 16 [Summer 1983], p. 45), and, before him, Gedalyahu Alon (*Studies in the Jewish History of the Second Commonwealth and the Mishnaic-Talmudic Period* [Tel Aviv: Hakibbutz Hameuchad, 1957–58], p. 278 [Hebrew]), contended that the Western text represents the original. Later, Flusser and Shmuel Safrai published a substantial article detailing the basis of Alon and Flusser's claim: "Das Aposteldekret und die Noachitischen Gebote, in E. Brocke and H.-J. Borkenings, eds., *Wer Tora mehrt, mehrt Leben: Festgabe fur Heinz Kremers* (Neukirchen-Vluyn, 1986), 176–92.

[4] E.g., Didache 3:1–6.

[5] M. Avodah Zarah 2:1.

[6] M. Avot 5:9.

"Requirements for Gentiles" was abridged and adapted from the article, "The Apostolic Decree (Acts 15:20, 29; 21:25): Commandments for Gentiles?" by David Bivin, published electronically in the October 2004 issue of *Jerusalem Perspective Pipeline*.

22.

The Root of the Olive Tree

If the root is holy, so are the branches. But if some of the branches were broken off, and you, a wild olive shoot, were grafted in their place to share the richness of the olive tree, do not boast over the branches. If you do boast, remember it is not you that support the root, but the root that supports you. You will say, "Branches were broken off so that I might be grafted in." That is true. They were broken off because of their unbelief, but you stand fast only through faith. So do not become proud, but stand in awe. (Rom 11:16b-20, RSV)

The apostle Paul asserted in Romans 11:1 that God had not rejected his people. Speaking metaphorically, he went on to compare the people of Israel to a cultivated olive tree. Because of unbelief, some, but not all, of the tree's branches had been broken off, and a wild olive branch had been grafted to the stock.[1] Paul emphasized, however, that grafting the original branches back to the stock of the cultivated tree would be a much simpler task than grafting a wild olive to it.

Paul spoke about Israel as a "cultivated olive tree" whose rootage was in the Patriarchs, particularly Abraham.[2] Some Bible commentators, however, interpreted the root of the olive tree as Christ or his messianic program.[3] When making that claim, they came dangerously close to endorsing an old, rotten idea: the root represents the New Israel, that is, the Church.

Once an exegete has identified the root of Paul's metaphor with the Church, he or she cannot easily escape a subsequent and more pernicious conclusion: Israel of the flesh ceased to exist long ago. Rejecting carnal Israel, God gave her place of distinction to another. That other is the Church.

A massive olive tree over a thousand years old in the Garden of Gethsemane

The Messiah as the Root of the Tree

There are two reasons for interpreting the olive tree's root to symbolize the Messiah. First, the Greek word *riza* (root) appears in Romans 11:16. There *riza* seems to parallel the Greek word *aparche* (firstfruits), which calls to mind 1 Corinthians 15:20, 23. There Paul referred to Jesus, whom he regarded as Messiah, as the *aparche* — "the firstfruits of those who have fallen asleep."

The two parts of Romans 11:16, however, should be read both together and independently. The New Testament was first divided into verses in A.D. 1551. Always a time-saver when searching for a biblical passage, the versification of the text can also influence interpretation. In this case, verse 16a primarily belongs to the preceding discussion, where *aparche* refers to the first Jewish followers of Jesus.[4] In verse 11 Paul asked, "Have they stumbled so as to fall?" Verse 16a serves as one additional argument that this was not the case.

Paul's argument on behalf of his people includes an allusion to Numbers 15:17–21.[5] The Israelites had been commanded to present as an offering a baked loaf made from the firstfruits, or first portion, of the grain harvest. This loaf represented the entire seasonal grain crop. It, therefore, sanctified the whole harvest. The relatively small number of Jews who had accepted Jesus' messiahship were, figuratively speaking, the firstfruits of the Jewish nation. Like the special bread offering, they, too, sanctified the whole. For Paul, these few who had believed the gospel message proved that the Jewish nation had not been rejected. Its "fall" was neither complete nor final. God had not abandoned his people in favor of another.

Paul concluded his thoughts about Israel's status with his metaphor of the first portion of the dough. Despite Israel's stumbling, the faithfulness of a portion of the nation had beneficial spiritual implications for their unbelieving brethren.[6] At that point, Paul shifted gears and began accelerating in a new direction. With the division of the text into verses in the sixteenth century, henceforth this change in direction would start in the middle of verse 16.

The apostle now turned his attention to the Gentile believers in an effort to warn against misplaced pride.[7] He introduced the imagery of cultivated and wild olive trees. As part of that imagery, the stock's remaining natural branches represent the Jewish believers. In Paul's mind, both those Jews who had accepted Jesus' messianic claims and those who had not were the children of Abraham, the former through faith and physical lineage, but the latter only through physical lineage. The stock was holy, and therefore, so also were all of the natural branches. But some of the natural branches had been broken off, and a wild olive had been grafted to the stock. The wild branch benefited from the stock and, like the natural branches, was now holy, too.

The second and more influential reason for wrongly interpreting Paul's metaphorical "root" as the Messiah was due to another passage, where Paul referred to the messianic title "the root of Jesse." In Romans 15:12, the apostle quoted from the prophet Isaiah: "And in that day, there will be the root of Jesse, and the one who will arise to rule over nations. The nations will hope in him" (Is 11:10). Paul took his quotation from the Greek Septuagint. The Hebrew Masoretic text reads: "In that day, the root of Jesse that has remained standing will become an ensign to [the] peoples. Him [the] nations will seek." Apparently impressed by Paul's initiative, the author of the Book of Revelation referred to Jesus as the "root of David" (Rev 5:5; 22:16).

In Isaiah 11 the "root of Jesse" appears twice, once in verse 1, and again in verse 10. In Romans 15:12, Paul opted to quote from the less clear verse 10, which seems to indicate that the "root of Jesse" will arise to become a ruler over the nations. Verse 10 probably caught Paul's attention because of the word "nations," or "Gentiles," which does not appear in verse 1. Paul wanted to underscore that the Messiah had come for both Jew and Gentile. Romans 15:9-12 is a string of proof texts accentuating the Messiah's coming for the second group.

Isaiah 11:10 cannot be read independently of Isaiah 11:1. Both traditional and modern Jewish biblical commentators have made frequent mention of this. For example, Radak[8] comments about "the root of Jesse" in verse 10: "This is the one who goes forth from 'the root of Jesse,' as it was said, 'And a branch will sprout from his roots' (vs. 1), for Jesse is the root. And so we read in Targum Jonathan, 'a son of Jesse's son.'"[9] More recently, Amos Hacham commented on verse 10: "'The root of Jesse,' which grew and became a tree, as it was said above in verse 1: 'And a branch will sprout from his roots.'"[10] The phrase "root of Jesse" functions as an abbreviated form of "a branch from the root of Jesse." It is the shoot (hoter) or branch (netzer) – and not the stump or root – that symbolizes a future messianic figure.

Paul must have understood Isaiah 11:10 as have traditional and modern Jewish exegetes. According to Luke, Paul alluded to Isaiah 11:1, 10 while preaching a sermon in a synagogue at Pisidian Antioch (Acts 13:23). He described Jesus as a savior descending from the offspring of Jesse. Here the offspring would have corresponded to Jesse's root, from which Jesus the branch sprouted.[11]

To read Romans 11:16b-24 alongside Romans 15:12 without properly considering Isaiah 11:1, 10 can easily lead to unsatisfactory conclusions. The "root of Jesse" should not be equated with the holy root of the olive tree. Although verse 10 speaks metaphorically of the "root of Jesse," this verse must be read in the light of verse 1. "Root of Jesse" in verse 10 actually refers to the branch that sprouts forth from the root of Jesse.

If while writing Romans 11:16b-24, Paul was not thinking of Isaiah 11:10, whence did he derive his imagery? Consider Jeremiah 11:16, where the prophet spoke of a fair olive tree whose branches were in danger of being broken. According to the Hebrew Masoretic tradition, the prophet declared:

> The LORD [once] called you "a green olive tree, fair, with choice fruit." But with a great roaring sound he will set it on fire, and its branches will be broken.

The Greek Septuagintal version of Jeremiah 11:16 reads differently:

> The Lord called your name "a fair olive tree of a goodly shade in appearance." At the noise of its being lopped, fire was kindled against it. Great is the affliction coming upon you. Her branches have become useless.

Regardless of which text, the Hebrew or the Greek, Paul had in mind, the imagery is consistent with that of Romans 11:17. Paul knew well both Hebrew and Greek, and he read Scripture in both languages. To restrict him to one version over and against another would not do justice to Paul's bicultural background. In this case, however, even if he had been thinking only of the Septuagint, he still could have based Romans 11:17 on Jeremiah 11:16.

In Jeremiah's allegory, the olive tree apparently symbolized the people of Israel. As an olive tree, the prophet metaphorically spoke of the house of Israel (v. 10), of the people (v. 14), and of God's beloved (v. 15). Interestingly, in Romans 11:28, Paul spoke of Israel as being beloved. The apostle seems to have followed the prophet's lead in comparing the Jewish people to an olive tree. Paul was neither the first nor the last to make such a comparison. Jeremiah had done the same in the sixth century B.C., and the rabbis of the talmudic period happily kept the tradition alive.[12]

---

[1] Other rabbinic sources used the metaphor of Gentiles being grafted in as branches into the tree of Israel. Christian Maurer mentioned the rabbinic saying, "The two beautiful sprigs which God engrafted into Abraham are Ruth and Naomi [sic, Naamah], who let themselves be planted into Israel as proselytes," (entry *riza* in *Theological Dictionary of the New Testament,* ed. Gerhard Friedrich, trans. Geoffrey W. Bromiley [Grand Rapids, MI: Eerdmans, 1968], 6:987). Maurer refers to Rabbi Eleazar's saying preserved in b. Yevamot 63a: "What is the meaning of, 'And in you will all the families of the earth be blessed' [Gen 12:3]? The Holy One, Blessed Be He, said to Abraham: 'I have two branches to

engraft upon you: Ruth the Moabitess and Naamah the Ammonitess.' 'All the families of the earth.' [This scriptural phrase means that] even the other families who dwell on the earth are not blessed except for Israel's sake...." According to Joseph Shulam, the apostle Paul "uses the metaphor of 'grafting in' to graphically demonstrate God's plan to bless all the nations of the world through Abraham" (*A Commentary on the Jewish Roots of Romans* [Baltimore, MD: Lederer, 1997], pp. 363, 370).

[2] Chrisitan Maurer, *TDNT*, 6:989; Shulam, *Romans*, pp. 363, 371–73. Romans 11:28 helps to confirm that Paul had the Patriarchs in mind.

[3] E.g., in ancient times, the church fathers; in this century, Karl Barth: *Die Kirchliche Dogmatik*. Vol. 2: *Die Lehre von Gott*, part 2, 1942, p. 314 (English trans.: *Church Dogmatics* [Edinburgh: T. & T. Clark, 1957], pp. 285f.).

[4] Paul used *aparche* (firstfruits) in this sense in Rom 16:5 and 1 Cor 16:15.

[5] Compare Nehemiah 10:37; Ezekiel 44:30.

[6] Benefit accrues to the Jewish people as a whole thanks to the faithfulness of Jewish believers in Jesus! The firstfruits makes the whole holy (vs. 16a).

[7] There may have existed masked anti-Jewish sentiment among the Gentile members of the church at Rome. These Gentile believers gladly took advantage of the privileges granted by the Roman government to the Jewish religion, but at the same time wished to be viewed as distinct from the Jewish community. See Marcel Simon, Verus Israel: *A Study of the Relations between Christians and Jews in the Roman Empire (AD 135–425)*, translated from French by H. McKeating (Oxford: Oxford University Press, 1986), pp. 100–101. See also Harry J. Leon, *The Jews of Ancient Rome* (Philadelphia: Jewish Publication Society of America, 1960), pp. 9–11, 22, 45. According to Leon, it was only during the brutal persecution of Christians that followed the great fire of A.D. 64 that Roman authorities began to differentiate between Jews and Christians of the city (p. 28). For official documents from the first two centuries B.C. and the first half of the first century A.D. guaranteeing Jews of the Mediterranean world the right to observe their religious customs, and other privileges, see Josephus, Antiq. 14:185–267; 19:279–291.

[8] An acronym for Rabbi David Kimhi, a Bible commentator and grammarian who lived in southern France in the late twelfth and early thirteenth centuries.

[9] Targum Onkelos has the identical Aramaic translation. Both Onkelos and Jonathan interpreted "the root of Jesse" as "the son of Jesse." Both targums rendered vs. 1, "And a king will come forth from the sons of Jesse, and the Messiah from his sons' sons will be anointed." That is, both interpret "a shoot from the stump of Jesse" as "a king from the

sons of Jesse," and "a branch from his roots" as "the Messiah from his sons' sons." "The idea that the Messiah is the root of Jesse is common in the Synagogue. In this connection *shoresh* [Heb. "root"] is always related to the descendant of Jesse in the sense of shoot... This is supported by the general replacement of *shoresh* by the unequivocal *tsemah* 'shoot' [in the Targumim]" (Maurer, *TDNT*, 6:988).

[10] Amos Hacham, *The Book of Isaiah: Chapters 1–35* (Jerusalem: Mossad Harav Kook, 1984), p. 129 (Hebrew).

[11] I am indebted to Joseph Frankovic for pointing out to me the relevance of Acts 13:23. I also am indebted to him for his editorial suggestions and for the many discussions we have had about Romans 11.

[12] "R. Isaac said, At the time of the destruction of the Temple the Holy One, blessed be He, found Abraham standing in the Temple. Said He, *'What hath My beloved to do in My house?'* [Jer. 11:15]. Abraham replied, 'I have come concerning the fate of my children'. Said He, 'Thy children sinned and have gone into exile'. 'Perhaps', said Abraham, 'they only sinned in error?' And He answered, *'She hath wrought lewdness'* [ibid.]. 'Perhaps only a few sinned?' *'With many'* [ibid.], came the reply. 'Still', he pleaded, 'Thou shouldst have remembered unto them the covenant of circumcision'. And He replied, *'The hallowed flesh is passed from thee'* [ibid.]. 'Perhaps hadst Thou waited for them they would have repented', he pleaded. And He replied, *'When thou doest evil, then thou rejoicest!'* [ibid.]. Thereupon he put his hands on his head and wept bitterly, and cried, 'Perhaps, Heaven forfend, there is no hope for them'. Then came forth a Heavenly Voice and said, *'The Lord called thy name a leafy olive-tree, fair with goodly fruit'* [Jer 11:16]: as the olive-tree produces its best only at the very end, so Israel will flourish at the end of time" (b. Menahot 53b; English translation by Eli Cashdan, in *The Babylonian Seder Kodashim: Volume I*, ed. Isidore Epstein [London: The Soncino Press, 1948], p. 321).

Postscript to
The Root of the Olive Tree

Consequences of the Wrong Interpretation of Scripture

One must view with apprehension the erroneous association that some Christians have made between Romans 11:17 and John 15:6. These two verses share the common image of branches. In John, the branches represent people not abiding in Christ. Having been cast off, these branches are gathered and burned. The branches in Romans 11 were not destroyed, but are waiting to be grafted back to the stock.

Introduced by Pope Innocent III (1198-1216) and executed chiefly by Dominicans and Franciscans, the Inquisition reached its zenith in Spain between 1474 and 1504 during the reign of the Christian king of Castile, Ferdinand V and his queen Isabella, the same king and queen who sent Christopher Columbus on his voyage of discovery.[1] With only brief interludes, the Inquisition continued until 1820!

In 1483 Ferdinand and Isabella appointed their confessor, Tomás de Torquemada (1420-1498), a prior of the Dominican Order, as Grand Inquisitor. It was Torquemada who organized the Spanish Inquisition, setting up ecclesiastical courts in various cities for the purpose of hunting down heretics (usually Conversos, Jews who converted to Christianity under duress and who had maintained contact with the Jewish community) and laying down guidelines for the prosecutors, or inquisitors. It also was Torquemada who was primarily responsible for the expulsion of the Jews from Spain in 1492.[2]

The courts of the Inquisition confiscated the property of those convicted of heresy. Initially, the assets seized became the property of the state, but, as time went on, they were channeled more and more to the courts themselves. This wealth fueled the machine of the Inquisition, giving the inquisitional tribunals tremendous power. Since the tribunals stood to reap great financial benefit if the accused were convicted, it became increasingly difficult for the accused to get an acquittal. In fact, within a short time, hardly anyone brought before these courts was acquitted — certainly not the rich!

The accused were convicted on the flimsiest of evidence. Heads of family were imprisoned and their lands confiscated. Large families were reduced to poverty overnight. From the 16th to the 18th centuries the economy of the once-prosperous Iberian Peninsula was ravaged due to the draconian measures of the Inquisition's courts. Until today Spain and Portugal have never regained their former glory.

The severest form of punishment meted out by the Inquisition's tribunals was burning at the stake. However, as an arm of the church, the courts were not permitted to carry out these executions. Therefore, they resorted to a 400-year-old legal fiction: the one sentenced to death was handed over to the secular authorities accompanied by a written appeal for mercy to which was appended a recommendation that, if the secular authorities felt compelled to execute, they should do so "without the effusion of blood." In other words, they should burn the victim. This manner of execution was justified by John 15:6: "If a man abide not in me, he is cast forth as a branch, and is withered; and men gather them, and cast them into the fire, and they are burned" (KJV).[3]

For those who conducted the Spanish Inquisition, those not "abiding in Christ" were the Conversos. If those false Christians were "the branches fit for burning" of John 15:6, they undoubtedly were also the "broken off" branches of Romans 11:17. Since God himself had broken off the branches mentioned in Romans 11, surely, the inquisitors must have thought, it was God's will that these deceivers confess their heresy and suffer their punishment. It made no difference to the lords of the Inquisition that the branches in John's Gospel were actually runners or sprigs (Gr. *klemata*) of a grapevine and not, as in Romans, branches (Gr. *kladoi*) of an olive tree.

The story of the perversion of John 15:6's interpretation should drive home to all Christians the importance of sound biblical scholarship and the enormous dangers inherent in wrongly interpreting Scripture.[4]

---

[1] See *Encyclopaedia Judaica* (Jerusalem: Keter Publishing House, 1972), 8:1380–1407; *The Oxford Dictionary of the Christian Church*, ed. F. L. Cross (London: Oxford University Press, 1958), pp. 694–95.

[2] *Enc. Jud.*, 15:1264–5; *Oxford Dictionary*, pp. 1367–8.

[3] *Enc. Jud.*, 8:1404.

[4] I view myself as the descendant of those who took part in the Crusades, and carried out the Inquisition and other atrocities against the Jewish people. I wrote the Postscript to this chapter as a personal reminder to be vigilant lest I repeat the sins of my Christian ancestors. I believe that, as a Christian, I dare not have the attitude, "If I had lived in

the days of my fathers, I would not have taken part with them in shedding the blood of the prophets" (see Mt 23:30). Rather, I must accept responsibility for my Christian ancestors' sins, vow not to repeat them, express my sorrow to the Jewish people, and in any and every way possible, make restitution for these sins.

I realize that it is easy for me, living in a more enlightened age, to criticize my Christian predecessors, yet I know that it is my responsibility to denounce Christian anti-Semitism, past and present. I must acknowledge the anti-Semitic attitudes and actions of these ancestors — they were more horrible than I am capable of describing — and vow to do all in my power to repair the great damage that has been done. It may be unfair for a twentieth-century citizen of the United States, for example, to judge seventeenth- and eighteenth-century American slave-holders such as the United States' third president, Thomas Jefferson; nevertheless, slavery cannot be accepted or condoned. I am obligated to condemn both wrong thinking and sinful actions of earlier Christians towards the Jewish people, including church fathers such as Ignatius, Justin Martyr, Origen and John Chrysostom.

The inhumanity, the depravity, of Christian anti-Semitism cannot be excused — better to strongly condemn it than attempt the impossible task of justifying it. I feel scandalized and embarrassed by expressions of Christian anti-Semitism such as the Inquisition, the Crusades, outbreaks of anti-Jewish pogroms in eighteenth-, nineteenth- and early twentieth-century Russia and the Ukraine, and the Holocaust. I mourn the anti-Semitic words and deeds of my Christian forefathers. My hope is that I can learn from history and, with God's help, improve on my forefathers' sordid record, perhaps restoring in some small measure the church's broken relationship with the synagogue. Amen!

"The Root of the Olive Tree" was adapted from the article, "Romans 11: The Olive Tree's Root," by David Bivin, which is available online at www.JerusalemPerspective.com.

Glossary

Amidah (ah-mee-DAH; lit. "standing") The central prayer in Jewish life and liturgy that is said while standing (as its name indicates). Also known as the *shmoneh esreh* (shmo-NEH es-REY), meaning "eighteen," because the prayer originally consisted of eighteen benedictions. Sometimes called simply *Tefillah* (teh-fee-LAH, "prayer'), because it is the prayer par excellence.

Apocrypha (ah-POK-ruh-fuh) Books included in the Greek Septuagint and Vulgate translations of the Hebrew Bible but excluded from the Protestant canon. They largely reflect the thinking of the intertestamental era, sometimes shedding light on the Judaism of Jesus' time. (Adj. apocryphal)

Aramaic A northwest Semitic language closely related to Hebrew that was spoken in Israel along with Greek and Mishnaic Hebrew during Jesus' lifetime.

Bet Midrash (bet mid-RASH; lit. "house of study") Center for study and teaching of the Torah. In the first century, the *bet midrash* was usually connected to a synagogue, and learning took place in the synagogue's assembly hall or in a room adjoining it.

Bet Sefer (lit. "house of the book") First-century Jewish elementary school that was part of the synagogue, where boys between five and thirteen years learned the Scriptures and interpretation of them.

Dead Sea Scrolls Approximately 800 texts found in caves of the Judean desert near the Dead Sea that were written in Hebrew, Aramaic, or Greek and date from 250 B.C. to A.D. 68.. They contain the oldest known translations of the Hebrew Scriptures as well as documents of the Essene sect at Qumran.

Diaspora (die-A-spor-a) The area outside the land of Israel settled by Jews, or the Jews who settled there.

Essenes Sect of Jews of the Second Temple period that isolated themselves, lived ascetically, and referred to themselves as the "Sons of Light," in contrast to the "Sons of Darkness" – sinners and political enemies. The Dead Sea Scrolls contain the writings of this sect, along with copies of the Scriptures and other works.

Haggadah (hah-gah-DAH; also *aggadah,* ah-gah-DAH) Storytelling, like parables or midrash. Explaining the Bible and theology using story. Often contrasted with *halachah,* legal rulings (see next entry). In the Passover Seder, each participant reads from a book called the *Haggadah.*

Halachah (hah-lah-KHAH; pl. *halachot,* hah-lah-KHOTE) Law, regulation; the legal ruling on a particular issue; the body of Jewish law, especially the legal part of rabbinic literature. Often contrasted with *haggadah,* rabbinic parables and stories. (Adj. *halachic* (ha-LAH-kik) – pertaining to *halachah.*

Haluk (hah-LUK) A light linen tunic worn next to the skin, the inner of the two garments worn by first-century Jews.

Hasid (hah-SEED; lit. "pious one;" pl. *Hasidim,* hah-see-DEEM) A member of a sect of charismatic sages of the Second Temple period who shared the Pharisees' ethical values, but also were characterized by a familiarity with God and a greater emphasis on deeds than study of Torah. (Adj. *Hasidic,* hah-SIH-dik). Jesus' ministry had much in common with that movement.

Hebrew Bible (or, Hebrew Scriptures) Term favored by David Bivin to refer to the Scriptures shared by Jews and Christians, as opposed to the name "Old Testament."

Kal Vahomer (kal va-HOH-mer; lit. "light and heavy") A term of logic applied to the inference from minor to major, often including the phrase "How much more...." Jesus was one of many rabbinic teachers who used this form of logic.

Kalah Kahamurah (kah-LAH kah-hah-moo-RAH; lit. light as heavy) Rabbinic approach which stressed that less serious laws are no less significant than more serious laws. Jesus used this approach when he equated lust with adultery and anger with murder.

Malchut Shamayim (mahl-CHOOT shah-MAH-yeem; lit. "Kingdom of Heaven") Rabbinic term used in the Second Temple period to describe God's activity and reign over those who enthrone him as king, or when God takes control of a life or situation (*malchut*, kingship or reign; *shamayim*, heaven — a respectful euphemism for God). Exactly the same as "Kingdom of God." Matthew generally uses "Kingdom of Heaven"; Mark and Luke, "Kingdom of God."

Masoretic Text Text of the Hebrew Bible as punctuated and furnished with vowel points by the Masoretes, Jewish scholars of the sixth to ninth centuries A.D. It is the basis of all modern texts of the Hebrew Scriptures.

Mezuzah (meh-zoo-ZAH, pl. *mezuzot,* meh-zoo-ZOTE) The Hebrew word for doorpost, *mezuzah*, which also came to mean the encased parchment scroll inscribed with Deuteronomy 6:4–9 and 11:13–21 that is affixed to the gate and right-hand doorjambs of a Jewish home.

Midrash (meed-RAHSH, pl. *midrashim,* meed-rah-SHEEM) A rabbinic interpretation or expansion of a Bible text with a story to explain the passage. The term can also be applied to a collection of such expositions. (adj. *midrashic*)

Mishnah (mish-NAH, lit. "repetition," from the Hebrew root *sh-n-h*, to repeat.) The collection of Oral Torah (rabbinic rulings and sayings) compiled and committed to writing around A.D. 200. The Mishnah records the sayings of sages who lived and taught during the previous several hundred years, both before and after the time of Jesus.

Mishnaic Hebrew The Hebrew spoken in the land of Israel during the first centuries B.C./A.D., used loosely to refer to post-biblical Hebrew. Since this dialect was used in the rabbinic works composed during the following centuries, it also is referred to as "rabbinic Hebrew." Some scholars prefer the term "Middle Hebrew."

Mitzvah (meetz-VAH; lit. "commandment") Usually used in the sense of "religious obligation" or "good deed." Pl. *mitzvot,* mitz-VOTE.

Oral Torah In contrast to the Written Torah, which consists of the five books of Moses, the Oral Torah is the rabbinic interpretations and rulings based on the written Torah. For hundreds of years it was preserved only in oral form (see entry "Mishnah" above). In Judaism, the Oral Torah is considered just as inspired and binding as the written Torah.

Pericope (per-IH-koh-pee) An episode or story unit in the Synoptic Gospels; a division of a synopsis (pl. *pericopae*).

Pharisee A member of a lay movement of the Second Temple period which sought to revive religious practice and study of Torah. Although Jesus often seemed to conflict with them, his interpretation of Scripture was actually quite similar to theirs.

Pirke Avot (peer-KAY ah-VOTE; lit. "Chapters of the Fathers") A tractate of the Mishnah that contains rabbinic sayings, many of which are parallel to sayings of Jesus.

Post-biblical Term used by scholars to refer to the time after the writing of the Hebrew Bible. For Jewish scholars the New Testament would be considered post-biblical.

Pseudepigrapha (soo-duh-PIG-ruh-fuh; lit. "falsely written") A title for various pseudonymous or anonymous Jewish writings of the third century B.C. to the second century A.D. not found in the Hebrew Bible or Apocrypha.

R. An abbreviation used in rabbinic literature for the honorific titles, "Rabbi," "Rabban," "Rav" and "Rabbenu."

Rabbah Attached to the name of a book of the Bible, "Genesis Rabbah," for instance, it refers to a collection of commentary and midrash on that book.

Rabbi A respectful form of address meaning "my master" or "my teacher" that was used when speaking to teachers of the Scriptures in Jesus' day. Only after A.D. 70 did "Rabbi" become a formal title.

Second Temple Period Literally, the period from the rebuilding of the Temple (536–516 B.C.) to its destruction by the Romans in 70 A.D. However, the term often is meant to pertain to the latter part of this period, between 168 B.C. and A.D.135. Often used to refer to the time period of Jesus.

Septuagint The Greek translation of the Hebrew Scriptures completed in Egypt between approximately 250 and 100 B.C. (Adj. Septuagintal).

Shema (shmah; lit. "Hear") The first word of Deuteronomy 6:4, "Hear [*Shema*], O Israel! The LORD our God, the LORD is one." It actually refers to the recitation of three passages: Deuteronomy 6:4-9; 11:13-21; and Numbers 15:37-41. The *Shema* is regarded by Jews as the supreme affirmation of God's oneness and uniqueness.

Synoptic An adjective derived from *synopsesthai*, a Greek word meaning, "to view together, or at the same time"; specifically, the adjective refers to the first three Gospels of the New Testament.

Synoptic Gospels Matthew, Mark and Luke. The Synoptic Gospels (Matthew, Mark and Luke) are so similar in form and content that it is convenient to view them together. The three are often printed in parallel columns; such a book is called a synopsis. With the aid of a synopsis, the Synoptic Gospels can be studied synoptically, that is, studied by comparing the similarities and differences between them. The Gospel of John is so unlike the Synoptic Gospels that there is limited value in trying to view it "synoptically" with the other three Gospels.

Synoptic Problem The scholarly debate concerning the order in which the Synoptic Gospels were written and the literary sources used by each.

Talit (tah-LEET) The outer of the two garments worn by first-century Jews, a heavy mantle usually woven from wool. It was a large, rectangular piece of cloth, and had tassels (*tzitziyot*) at each of its four corners.

Talmud Large volume of commentary on the Mishnah. The commentary is printed section by section following each verse of the Mishnah. There are two Talmuds: the Jerusalem (or Palestinian) Talmud, which was completed about A.D. 400; and the Babylonian Talmud, which became authoritative, which was completed about a century later.

Targum An Aramaic translation of a portion of the Hebrew Scriptures (pl. *targumim* or *targums*). Since the inspired text could not be changed or altered in even the smallest way, the targum made possible the insertion of various explanations and clarifications that amplified the text.

Tefillin (teh-fee-LEEN) Small leather boxes worn on the forehead and arm to fulfill the words of Deut. 6:8. In Jesus' time, these were worn all day long, but in modern times are worn only during prayer.

Tetragrammaton The four-letter, divine name of God, usually transliterated as "YHWH."

Torah Hebrew for "teaching, instruction." Refers to the first five books of the Bible, also called the Pentateuch. *Torah* may also refer to the Oral Torah. Christians often translate *Torah* as "law," while Jewish translations usually render it "teaching."

Tosephta (lit. "addition, supplement") An early collection of rabbinic teaching that supplements the Mishnah.

Tzitzit (tsee-TSEET, pl. *tzitziyot*, tsee-tsee-YOTE) Tassels tied to the four corners of a garment to obey the command in Numbers 15:37. In Jesus' time, these tassels were tied to the four corners of the *talit*, the heavy woolen outer garment.

Zealots A sect of Jewish extremists during the Great Revolt (A.D. 66–73) who urged a war to the death against the Roman occupiers of the Land, and ruthlessly persecuted Jews who held more moderate views.

Bibliography

Abrahams, Israel. *Studies in Pharisaism and the Gospels.* Repr. New York: Ktav, 1967.

Albright, W. F., and C. S. Mann. *Matthew.* Anchor Bible 26. New York: Doubleday, 1971.

Alon, Gedalyahu. *Studies in the Jewish History of the Second Commonwealth and the Mishnaic-Talmudic Period.* Tel Aviv: Hakibbutz Hameuchad, 1957–58. (Hebrew).

Barth, Karl. *Die Kirchliche Dogmatik.* Vol. 2: *Die Lehre von Gott,* part part 2, 1942. (English trans.: *Church Dogmatics* Edinburgh: T. & T. Clark, 1957).

Bivin, David. "Hebraic Idioms in the Gospels." *Jerusalem Perspective* 22 (1989) 6–7.

_____. "Jesus in Judea." *Jerusalem Perspective* 2 (1987) 1–2.

_____. "The New International Jesus." *Jerusalem Perspective* 56 (1999) 20–24.

Broshi, Magen. "Hatred: An Essene Religious Principle and Its Christian Consequences." *Antikes Judentum und Frühes Christentum.* Berlin: Walter de Gruyter (1999) 245–252.

Brown, Francis, S. R. Driver, and Charles Briggs. *The New Brown-Driver-Briggs-Gesenius Hebrew and English Lexicon.* Peabody, MA: Hendrickson, 1979.

Buth, Randall. "Jesus' Most Important Title." *Jerusalem Perspective* 25 (1990) 11–15.

_____. "Aramaic Language." *Dictionary of New Testament Background,* Craig Evans and Stanley Porter, eds. Downers Grove: Intervarsity (2000) 86–91.

Cohen, Abraham. *Everyman's Talmud.* New York: Schocken, 1975.

Cross, F. L., ed. *Oxford Dictionary of the Christian Church.* London: Oxford University Press, 1958.

Davies, W. D., and Dale C. Allison, Jr. *A Critical and Exegetical Commentary on the Gospel According to Saint Matthew.* International

Critical Commentary. Edinburgh: T&T Clark, 1988–1991.

Encyclopaedia Judaica. Jerusalem: Keter, 1972.

Epstein, Isidore. *The Babylonian Seder Kodashim: Volume I*. English translation by Eli Cashdan. London: Soncino, 1948.

Epstein, J. N. *Introduction to Tannaitic Literature: Mishna, Tosephta and Halakhic Midrashim*. Jerusalem: Magnes Press; and Tel Aviv: Dvir, 1957. (Hebrew).

Even-Shoshan, Abraham, ed. *A New Concordance of the Bible*. Jerusalem: Kiryath Sepher, 1987. (Hebrew).

Flusser, David, and Shmuel Safrai. "Das Aposteldekret und die Noachitischen Gebote." E. Brocke and H.-J. Borkenings, eds., *Wer Tora mehrt, mehrt Leben: Festgabe fur Heinz Kremers*. Vluyn: Neukirchen, 1986.

Flusser, David. "The Jewish-Christian Schism, Part I." *Immanuel* 16 (1983) 45.

_____. *Jesus*. 3rd ed. Jerusalem: Magnes Press, 2001.

_____. *Jewish Sources in Early Christianity*. New York: Adama Books, 1987.

_____. *Judaism and the Origins Of Christianity*. Jerusalem: Magnes Press, 1988.

Foakes-Jackson F. J., and K. Lake. 5 vols. *The Acts of the Apostles*. London: Macmillan, 1920–33.

Frymer-Kensky, Tikva, D. Novak, P. Ochs, D. F. Sandmel, M. A. Signer, eds. *Christianity in Jewish Terms*. Boulder: Westview Press, 2000.

Gundry, Robert H. *Matthew: A Commentary on His Handbook for a Mixed Church under Persecution*. 2nd ed.; Grand Rapids: Eerdmans, 1994.

Hacham, Amos. *The Book of Isaiah: Chapters 1–35*. Jerusalem: Mossad Harav Kook, 1984. (Hebrew).

Hagner, Donald. *Matthew*. Word Bible Commentary 33A–33B. Dallas: Word Books, 1993–1995.

Hartman, Louis F. "Names of God." *Encyclopaedia Judaica*. Jerusalem: Keter (1971) 7:674–85.

Lachs, Samuel Tobias. *A Rabbinic Commentary on the New Testament: The Gospels of Matthew, Mark and Luke*. Hoboken: Ktav, 1987.

Leon, Harry J. *The Jews of Ancient Rome*. Philadelphia: Jewish Publication

Society of America, 1960.

Liddell, Henry George, and Robert Scott. *A Greek-English Lexicon*. Revised and augmented by Henry Stuart Jones with Roderick McKenzie. Oxford: Clarendon Press, 1968.

Lindsey, Robert. *The Jesus Sources: Understanding the Gospels*. Tulsa: HaKesher, 1990.

_____. *Jesus Rabbi & Lord: The Hebrew Story of Jesus Behind Our Gospels*. Oak Creek, WI: Cornerstone Publishing, 1990.

_____. "Four Keys for Better Understanding Jesus." *Jerusalem Perspective* 49 (1995) 10-17, 38.

Manson, T. W. *The Sayings of Jesus*. London: SCM, 1974.

Maurer, Christian. "*Riza*." *Theological Dictionary of the New Testament*. Vol. 6. Ed. Gerhard Friedrich, trans. Geoffrey W. Bromiley. Grand Rapids: Eerdmans, 1968, 985-90.

Metzger, Bruce M. *A Textual Commentary on the Greek New Testament*. London: United Bible Societies, 1975.

Montefiore, Claude. *The Religion of Yesterday and Tomorrow* 1925.

_____. *The Synoptic Gospels*. 2nd ed. 2 vols. London: Macmillan, 1927.

Montefiore, Claude and Herbert Loewe. *A Rabbinic Anthology*. New York: Schocken, 1974.

Myers, Philip Van Ness. *Rome: Its Rise and Fall*. 2nd ed. Boston: Ginn and Company, 1901.

Nolland, John. "The Gospel Prohibition of Divorce: Tradition History and Meaning." *Journal for the Study of the New Testament* 58 (1995) 19-35.

Nun, Mendel. "Let Down Your Nets." *Jerusalem Perspective* 24 (1990) 11-13.

Pritz, Ray. "The Divine Name in the Hebrew New Testament." *Jerusalem Perspective* 31 (1991) 10-12.

Safrai, Shmuel. "Education and the Study of Torah." *The Jewish People in the First Century*. Eds. Shmuel Safrai and Menahem Stern. Amsterdam: Van Gorcum, 1976, 945-70.

_____. "Jesus and the Hasidim." *Jerusalem Perspective* 42, 43 & 44 (1994) 3-22.

_____. "Literary Languages in the Time of Jesus." *Jerusalem Perspective* 31 (1991) 3-8.

_____. "Religion in Everyday Life." in *The Jewish People in the First Century*. Eds. Shmuel Safrai and Menahem Stern. Amsterdam: Van Gorcum, 1976, 793-833.

_____. "Talmudic Literature as an Historical Source for the Second Temple Period." *Mishkan*. 17-18 (1993) 121-37.

_____. "Teaching of Pietists in Mishnaic Literature." *The Journal of Jewish Studies*. 16 (1956) 15-33.

Santala, Risto. *The Messiah in the Old Testament in the Light of Rabbinical Writings*. Jerusalem: Keren Ahvah Meshihit, 1993.

Schürer, Emil. *The History of the Jewish People in the Age of Jesus Christ*. G. Vermes, F. Millar and M. Black, eds. 3 vols. Edinburgh: T & T Clark, 1973.

Shulam, Joseph. *A Commentary on the Jewish Roots of Romans*. Baltimore: Lederer, 1997.

Silverman, Godfrey Edmond. "Galatinus, Pietro (Petrus) Columna." *Encyclopaedia Judaica*. 7:262-63.

Simon, Marcel. Verus Israel: *A Study of the Relations between Christians and Jews in the Roman Empire (AD 135-425)*. Trans. by H. McKeating. Oxford: Oxford University Press, 1986.

Smith, Morton. "Mt. 5:43: 'Hate Thine Enemy.'" *Harvard Theological Review*. 45 (1952) 71-3.

Stendahl, Krister. "Hate, Non-Retaliation, and Love." *Harvard Theological Review* 55 (1962) 343-55.

Taylor, Vincent. *The Gospel According to St. Mark*. London: Macmillan, 1952.

Theological Dictionary of the New Testament. 10 vols. Eds. Gerhard Kittel (vols. 1-4); Gerhard Friedrich (vols. 5-10). Grand Rapids: Eerdmans, 1964-1976.

Theological Dictionary of the Old Testament. Eds. G. J. Botterweck and H. Ringgren. Grand Rapids: Eerdmans, 1974ff.

Tolstoy, Leo. *The Kingdom of God Is within You*. Trans. Constance Garnett. Repr. Lincoln: University of Nebraska Press, 1984.

Weiss, Konrad. "*Phortion*." *Theological Dictionary of the New Testament*. Vol. 9. Ed. Gerhard Friedrich, trans. Geoffrey W. Bromiley. Grand Rapids:

Eerdmans, 1974, 84-7.

Williams, Charles B. *The New Testament: A Private Translation in the Language of the People.* Chicago: Moody Press, 1958.

Wilson, Marvin. *Our Father Abraham.* Grand Rapids: Eerdmans, 1989.

Wise, Michael, and Martin Abegg. *The Dead Sea Scrolls, A New Translation.* San Francisco: HarperCollins, 1999.

Yadin, Yigael. *Tefillin from Qumran.* Jerusalem: Israel Exploration Society, 1969.

Young, Brad H. *Jesus the Jewish Theologian.* Peabody, MA: Hendrickson, 1995.

Index

About the Author

David Bivin, a specialist in the Semitic and Jewish background of the Gospels, is a member of the Jerusalem School of Synoptic Research, a think tank made up of Jewish and Christian scholars dedicated to better understanding the Synoptic Gospels.

A native of Cleveland, Oklahoma, Bivin has lived in Israel since 1963, when he came to Jerusalem on a Rotary Foundation Fellowship to do postgraduate work at the Hebrew University. He remained at the Hebrew University until 1969 studying Jewish history and literature under professors Menahem Stern, David Flusser, Shmuel Safrai and Yechezkel Kutscher, and archaeology under professors Yigael Yadin, Yohanan Aharoni and Michael Avi-Yonah. During those six years, and for many years afterwards, he also studied privately with Jerusalem scholar-pastor Robert L. Lindsey.

From 1970 to 1981 Bivin directed the Hebrew Language Division of the American Ulpan, and the Modern Hebrew Department of the Institute of Holy Land Studies (later renamed Jerusalem University College). He is author of the video language course, *Aleph-Bet: A Beginner's Introduction to Reading and Writing Hebrew.*

In 1982 Bivin coauthored, with Roy Blizzard, Jr., *Understanding the Difficult Words of Jesus.* This was the first attempt to write a non-scholarly account of the pioneering work of Robert Lindsey, David Flusser and their students in Jerusalem. The book has now been translated into German, French, Japanese, Spanish, Portuguese, and Polish.

For twelve years (1987–1999) Bivin published *Jerusalem Perspective*, a print magazine that presented the life and teachings of Jesus in their original cultural and linguistic settings. In 2000 the magazine was replaced by "Jerusalem Perspective Online" (http://www.jerusalemperspective.com), a Web site dedicated to the exploration of Jewish background to the life and words of Jesus.

The En-Gedi Resource Center

En-Gedi is the name of the oasis in the desert of southern Israel where David fled to escape from King Saul. There, water gushes from rocky cliffs in springs and waterfalls, and any place it touches is covered with lush greenery, while only yards away, the harsh desert is parched and lifeless. The springs of En-Gedi are a powerful image of "living water" as the presence of God. This picture of God's Spirit is found throughout the Scriptures.

Just like the land of Israel, the Scriptures can be somewhat "dry and dusty" when we don't understand the language, imagery and cultural setting that they came from. When we do, all of a sudden God's word refreshes our souls and makes us grow in ways we never imagined.

With these thoughts in mind, the En-Gedi Resource Center seeks to be a source of living water, offering a Spirit-filled understanding of the Scriptures that will help Christians grow and bear fruit as disciples of Jesus. The purpose of this book and of our ministry is to help others see Jesus with greater clarity, by placing him back into his original language, culture and religious environment.

Our goal is not just to gain greater factual knowledge, but to develop a richer, deeper relationship with Jesus, and a commitment to becoming better disciples of him. We believe that Jesus' commands, high calling, and challenge to us are never clearer than when we hear him through the ears of his first listeners.

* * * * * * *

For more about our ministry, see EnGediResourceCenter.com or write us at: P.O. Box 1971, Holland, MI 49422–1971, USA

We invite you to continue learning at our website. Visit EnGediResourceCenter.com for a glossary and help page, articles, Bible commentaries, and a bookstore with related resources. If you would like to receive articles and news by email, you can sign up there as well.

Your feedback on this book is welcome. See the website to order additional copies, with group discounts available.

Also available from En-Gedi:

Listening to the Language of the Bible:
Hearing It Through Jesus' Ears

by Lois Tverberg & Bruce Okkema

An introduction to the rich Hebrew words and Jewish ideas that deepen Bible study, with more than 60 brief, illustrated devotional articles that unpack the meaning of a biblical word or phrase for our lives. A Companion Bible Study is also available. See EnGediResourceCenter.com for details.

The En-Gedi Resource Center is currently managed by its founder, Lois Tverberg, as a division of Living Water Books, LLC. Financial gifts are appreciated, but resources purchased from the En-Gedi website support this ministry too. For the latest news about Lois' writing, visit OurRabbiJesus.com.

En-Gedi Resource Center
P.O. Box 1971
Holland, MI 49422–1971